SHAKESPEARE
FOR CSEC

William Shakespeare

TWELFTH NIGHT

with CSEC notes

Volume consultants:

Carol Clarke

Simone Gibbs

Arlene Kasmally-Dwarika

OXFORD
UNIVERSITY PRESS

Contents

Preface

The very name *Shakespeare* can overwhelm: so many associations with culture and history. We hope you will approach the plays with curiosity and a willingness to embrace the strangeness of Shakespeare's world: those quaint ways, weapons and words!

Our aim in the **Shakespeare for CSEC** series is to provide a bridge between Shakespeare's world and our own. For all the differences between the two worlds it is intriguing to find so many similarities: parents and children; power games; loyalty and treachery; prejudice; love and hate; fantasy and reality; comedy and horror; the extremes of human behaviour. It is oddly moving to find that the concerns of the human race have not changed so much over the centuries, and that Shakespeare's themes are modern and recognisable.

The left-hand pages are intended to assist students and teachers in deeper appreciation of the text. Unfamiliar words and expressions are explained. There are ideas for guided discussion and focus as you proceed through each scene. Every scene has activities designed for individuals and groups, suitable for in-class and take-home tasks. Each act has a bulleted summary, for ease of reference and each scene has a summary that brings together the main developments of that scene.

At the beginning of the play there are two introductory essays, which discuss and analyse the major themes and encourage other ways of reading and interpreting the text. At the end of the text, there are opportunities to explore the play in the classroom with a series of activities along with twenty essay questions designed to prepare students for the CSEC examinations.

You'll notice that there are a series of photos throughout the book. These are from the beautiful Twelfth Night production by the Oratory Foundation at the Naparima Bowl in Trinidad. Context is everything and productions like this with the added benefit of a Caribbean signature show us the continued relevance of Shakespeare to everyone.

Our aim is that you finish the play enthused and intrigued, and eager to explore more of Shakespeare's works. We hope you will begin to see that although ideally the plays are experienced in performance, there is also a place for reading together and discussing as a class, or for simply reading them privately to yourself.

Carol Clarke and **Simone Gibbs**

Foreword

Who bothers to read introductions, especially introductions to plays by Shakespeare?

Well, you do, obviously, and that's a good start if you want to get more from your literature study. Reading this Foreword will help you to get more from Shakespeare's writing and from the accompanying material provided with the play.

Shakespeare – the great adapter

Shakespeare is regarded as a great writer but not because he was an original inventor of stories. His plays are nearly all adaptations of stories he found in books, or in history – or in somebody else's play. His originality came from the way he used this material. He changed his sources to suit himself and his audiences and was never afraid to change the facts if they didn't suit him.

The best way of understanding what Shakespeare thought valuable in a story is to look at the way he altered what he found.

The **Introductory Essays** show how he changed characters or timescales to enhance the dramatic effect or to suit a small cast of actors.

Shakespeare – the great realist

What Shakespeare added to his source material was his insight into people and society. He understood what makes people tick and what makes society hold together or fall apart. He showed how people behave – and why – by showing their motives and their reactions to experiences such as love, loss, dreams, fears, threats and doubts. These have not changed, even if we think science and technology make us different from people in Shakespeare's day. He was also realistic. He avoided stereotypes, preferring to show people as a complex mixture of changing emotions.

When you use the character sheets provided by your teacher, you will see this realism in action. His characters behave differently in different circumstances, and they change over time – just as we do in real life.

Shakespeare – the language magician

Shakespeare's cleverness with language is not just his ability to write beautiful poetry. He also wrote amusing dialogue, common slang, rude insults and the thoughts of people under pressure. He wrote script that uses the sounds of words to convey emotion, and the associations of words to create vivid images in our heads.

When you use the glossary notes you will see how his language expresses ugliness, hatred, suspicion, doubt and fear as well as happiness, beauty and joy.

Shakespeare – the theatrical innovator

Theatre before Shakespeare was different from today. Ordinary people enjoyed songs and simple shows, and educated people – the minority – enjoyed stories from Latin and Greek. Moral and religious drama taught right and wrong and there were spectacular masques full of music and dance for the audience to join in. Shakespeare put many of these elements together, so most people could expect something to appeal to them. He was an inclusive writer for a comprehensive audience, writing to please the educated and the uneducated. He was the first to put realistic people from every walk of life on stage – not just kings and generals, but characters who talked and behaved like the ordinary folk in the audience. He was less interested in right and wrong than in the comedy or tragedy of what people actually do. *Everybody Loves Raymond,* and *The Haves and the Have Nots,* are dramas which follow a trend started by Shakespeare over four hundred years ago. He managed this in theatres which lacked lighting, sound amplification, scene changes, curtains or a large cast of actors.

The performance features accompanying the play text will help to show you how Shakespeare's stagecraft is used to best dramatic effect.

The examination is designed to test your ability to respond to the following:

1. Shakespeare's ideas and themes

2. Shakespeare's use of language

3. Shakespeare's skill in writing for stage performance

4. The social, cultural and historical aspects of his plays

5. Different interpretations of the plays.

1. Showing personalities (ideas and themes)

Shakespeare thought drama should do more than preach simple moral lessons. He thought it should show life as it was, daft and serious, joyful and painful. He didn't believe in simple versions of good and evil, heroes and villains. He thought most heroes had unpleasant parts to their nature, just as most villains had good parts. This is why he showed people as a mixture. In *Hamlet,* he wrote that the dramatist should **hold a mirror up to nature**, so that all of us can see ourselves reflected. As he picks on the parts of human behaviour that don't change (fear, jealousy, doubt, self-pity), his characters remind us of people we know today – and of ourselves – not just people who lived a long time ago. This is because Shakespeare shows us more than his characters' status in life. He knew that beneath the robes or the crown there is a heart the same as any tradesman's or poor person's. He knew that nobody in real life is perfect – so he didn't put perfect characters on his stage.

Therefore, we see some imperfections even in characters we admire. Orsino is self-indulgent and has the potential to be vengeful; Olivia's self-absorption in mourning for her brother has the potential to alienate her; and Viola's male/female balancing act creates tension.

2a. Shakespeare's use of the English language (sound and image)

Shakespeare wrote the speech of uneducated servants and traders but he could also write great speeches using rhetoric. Whether it is a dim-witted inn-servant called Francis in *Henry IV Part One*, or a subtle political operator like Mark Antony in *Julius Caesar*, Shakespeare finds words to make them sound and seem convincing.

2b. Shakespeare's verse

Shakespeare's plays are mainly written in 'blank verse', the form preferred by most dramatists in the sixteenth and early seventeenth centuries. Blank verse has a regular rhythm, but does not rhyme. It is a very flexible medium, which is capable – like the human speaking voice – of a wide range of tones. Easily the best way to understand and appreciate Shakespeare's verse is to read it aloud – and don't worry if you don't understand everything! Try not to be influenced by the dominant rhythm. Instead, decide which are the most important words in each line and use the regular metre to drive them forward to the listeners. Shakespeare used a particular form of blank verse called iambic pentameter.

In iambic pentameter the lines are ten syllables long. Each line is divided into pairs of syllables, or 'feet'. Each 'foot' has one stressed and one unstressed syllable – a pattern that often appears in normal English speech. Here is an example:

> **Orsino**
> If músic bé the foód of lóve, play ón,
> Give mé excéss of ít, that, súrfeitíng,
> The áppetíte may sícken, ánd so díe.
> That stráin agáin, it hád a dýing fáll;
> O, ít came o'ér my éar like thé sweet soúnd
> That bréathes upón a bánk of vióléts,
> Stéaling and gíving ódour. Enóugh, no móre;
> 'Tis nót so sweét now ás it wás befóre.
> O spírit of lóve, how quíck and frésh art thóu,
> That nótwithstánding thý capácitý,
> Recéiveth ás the séa, nought énters thére,
> Of whát valíditý and pítch soé'er,
> But fálls intó abátement ánd low príce
> Evén in á minúte! So fúll of shápes is fáncy,

That ít alóne is hígh fantásticál.
Curio
Will yóu go húnt, my lórd?
Orsino

What, Cúrio?

Curio
The hárt.
Orsino
Why só I dó, the nóblest thát I háve.   (Act 1, Scene 1, lines 1–19)

Here the pentameter accommodates a variety of speech tones – the careful regularity of the first lines emphasizes Orsino's self-conscious pose as the romantic lover, delivering beautifully prepared thoughts. His lyrical ecstasy swoons over the 'bank of violets'; it is dismissed with the abrupt 'Enough, no more'; and then it develops into a highly philosophical meditation about the nature of love. Curio's suggestion, 'Will you go hunt, my lord?', brings a note of commonsense – perhaps even of exasperation! Orsino is quick to respond, sharing in the same pentameter as Curio.

In this quotation, the lines are mainly regular in length and normal in iambic stress pattern. Sometimes Shakespeare deviates from the norm, writing lines that are longer or shorter than ten syllables, and varying the stress patterns for unusual emphasis ('Stéaling and gíving ódour. Enoúgh, no móre'). The verse line sometimes contains the grammatical unit of meaning – "Tis nót so swéet now ás it wás befóre' – thus allowing for a pause at the end of the line, before a new idea is started; at other times, the sense runs on from one line to the next – 'thý capácitý Recéiveth ás the séa'. This makes for the natural fluidity of speech, avoiding monotony but still maintaining the iambic rhythm.

3a. Writing for a mixed audience (writing for stage performance)
As a popular dramatist who made his money by appealing to the widest range of people, Shakespeare knew that some of his audience would be literate, and some not. So he made sure that there was something for everybody – something clever and something vulgar, something comic and something tragic.

The rowdy and drunken behaviour of Sir Toby, the bawdy exchanges among Maria, Feste and Sir Toby, and the practical joke played on Malvolio all add to the high entertainment value of the drama.

3b. Shakespeare's craft (writing for stage performance)
Shakespeare worked with very basic stage technology but, as a former actor, he knew how to give his actors the guidance they needed. His scripts use embedded prompts, either to actors, or to the audience, so that he did not have to write stage directions for his actors. If an actor says, **Put your cap to**

its proper purpose, it is a cue to another actor to be using his hat for fancy gestures, rather than wearing it on his head. If an actor comes on stage and says, **So this is the forest of Arden** we know where the scene is set, without expensive props and scenery.

4. Social, cultural and historical aspects

There are two ways of approaching this. One way is to look at what the plays reveal for us about life in Shakespeare's time – and how it is different from today. The other is to look at what the plays reveal for us about life in Shakespeare's time – and how it is the same today.

The play might open up spaces for discussion on issues of class and gender. You might begin to ask who controls power, whether on the personal or political level. You might want to ask the extent to which these issues have changed in the 21st century.

5. Alternative interpretations

You can look at Shakespeare's play in its own time and in ours and sometimes see differences, and sometimes see similarities. Your literature study expects you to understand how Shakespeare can be interpreted by different people in different eras and in different places. It's important to have your own view of how the plays should be performed.

The notes and commentary throughout this edition will help you to form your own interpretation, and to understand how others might interpret differently. Look especially at references to how different stage and film productions have taken different approaches to the script that Shakespeare wrote.

Enjoy Shakespeare's play! It's your play, too!

Background

England in 1600

When Shakespeare was writing *Twelfth Night*, many people still believed that the sun went round the earth. They were taught that this was the way God had ordered things, and that – in England – God had founded a Church and appointed a monarchy so that the land and people could be well governed.

'The past is a foreign country; they do things differently there.'

L. P. Hartley

Government

For most of Shakespeare's life, the reigning monarch of England was Queen Elizabeth I. With her counsellors and ministers, she governed the nation from London, although fewer than half a million people out of a total population of six million lived in the capital city. In the rest of the country, law and order were maintained by the land-owners and enforced by their deputies. The average man had no vote, and women had no rights at all.

Religion

At this time, England was a Christian country. All children were baptised, soon after they were born, into the Church of England; they were taught the essentials of the Christian faith, and instructed in their duty to God and to humankind. Marriages and funerals were conducted only by the licensed clergy and according to the Church's rites and ceremonies. Attending divine service was compulsory; absences (without a good medical reason) could be punished by fines. By such means, the authorities were able to keep some control over the population – recording births, marriages, and deaths; being alert to anyone who refused to accept standard religious practices, who could be politically dangerous; and ensuring that people received the approved teachings through the official 'Homilies' which were regularly preached in all parish churches.

Elizabeth I's father, Henry VIII, had broken away from the Church of Rome, and from that time all people in England were able to hear the church services *in their own language* rather than in Latin. The Book of Common Prayer was used in every church, and an English traslation of the Bible was read aloud in public. The Christian religion had never been so well taught before!

Education

School education reinforced the Church's teaching. From the age of four, boys might attend the 'petty school' (its name came from the French '*petite école*' to learn reading and writing along with a few prayers; some schools also included work with numbers. At the age of seven, boys were ready for the grammar schools (if their fathers were willing and able to pay the fees).

Grammar schools taught Latin grammar, translation work and the study of Roman authors, paying attention as much to style as to content. The art of fine writing was therefore important from early youth. A very few students went on to university; these were either clever boys who won scholarships, or else the sons of rich noblemen. Girls stayed at home and learned domestic and social skills – cooking, sewing, perhaps even music. The lucky ones might learn to read and write.

Language

At the start of the 16th century the English had a very poor opinion of their own language: there was little serious writing in English, and hardly any literature. Latin was the language of international scholarship, and the eloquent style of the Romans was much admired. Many translations from Latin were made, and in this way writers increased the vocabulary of English and made its grammar more flexible. French, Italian, and Spanish works were also translated and, for the first time, there were English versions of the Bible. By the end of the century, English was a language to be proud of: it was rich in vocabulary, capable of infinite variety and subtlety, and ready for all kinds of word-play – especially *puns*, for which Elizabethan English is renowned.

Drama

The great art-form of the Elizabethan and Jacobean age was its drama. The Elizabethans inherited a tradition of play-acting from the Middle Ages, and they reinforced this by reading and translating the Roman playwrights. At the beginning of the 16th century plays were performed by groups of actors. These were all-male companies (boys acted the female roles) who travelled from town to town, setting up their stages in open places (such as inn-yards) or, with the permission of the owner, in the hall of some noble house. The touring companies continued outside London into the 17th century; but in London, in 1576, a new building was erected for the performance of plays. This was the Theatre, the first purpose-built playhouse in England. Other playhouses followed, including the Globe, where most of Shakespeare's plays were performed, and English drama reached new heights.

There were people who disapproved, of course. The theatres, which brought large crowds together, could encourage the spread of disease – and dangerous ideas. During the summer, when the plague was at its worst, the playhouses were closed. A constant censorship was imposed, more or less severe at different times. The Puritans, a religious and political faction who wanted to impose strict rules of behaviour, tried to close down the theatres. However, partly because the royal family favoured drama, and partly because the buildings were outside the city limits, they did not succeed until 1642.

Theatre

From contemporary comments and sketches – most particularly a drawing by a Dutch visitor, Johannes de Witt – it is possible to form some idea of the typical Elizabethan playhouse for which most of Shakespeare's plays were written. Hexagonal (six-sided) in shape, it had three roofed galleries encircling an open courtyard. The plain, high stage projected into the yard, where it was surrounded by the audience of standing 'groundlings'. At the back were two doors for the actors' entrances and exits; and above these doors was a balcony – useful for a musicians' gallery or for the acting of scenes 'above'. Over the stage was a thatched roof, supported on two pillars, forming a canopy – which seems to have been painted with the sun, moon, and stars for the 'heavens'.

Underneath was space (concealed by curtains) which could be used by characters ascending and descending through a trapdoor in the stage. Costumes and properties were kept backstage in the 'tiring house'. The actors used the most luxurious costumes they could find, often clothes given to them by rich patrons. Stage properties were important for showing where a scene was set, but the dramatist's own words were needed to explain the time of day, since all performances took place in the early afternoon.

A replica of Shakespeare's own theatre, the Globe, has been built in London, and stands in Southwark, almost exactly on the Bankside site of the original.

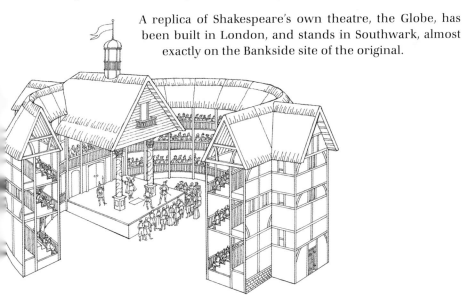

William Shakespeare, 1564–1616

Elizabeth I was Queen of England when Shakespeare was born in 1564. He was the son of a tradesman who made and sold gloves in the small town of Stratford-upon-Avon, and he was educated at the grammar school in that town. Shakespeare did not go to university when he left school, but worked, perhaps, in his father's business. When he was eighteen he married Anne Hathaway, who became the mother of his daughter, Susanna, in 1583, and of twins in 1585.

There is nothing exciting, or even unusual, in this story; and from 1585 until 1592 there are no documents that can tell us anything at all about Shakespeare. But we have learned that in 1592 he was known in London, and that he had become both an actor and a playwright.

We do not know when Shakespeare wrote his first play, and indeed we are not sure of the order in which he wrote his works. If you look on page 108 at the list of his writings and their approximate dates, you will see how he started by writing plays on subjects taken from the history of England. No doubt this was partly because he was always an intensely patriotic man – but he was also a very shrewd businessman. He could see that the theatre audiences enjoyed being shown their own history, and it was certain that he would make a profit from this kind of drama.

The plays in the next group are mainly comedies, with romantic love stories of young people who fall in love with one another, and at the end of the play marry and live happily ever after. *Twelfth Night* is the last of these.

At the end of the 16th century the happiness disappears, and Shakespeare's plays become melancholy, bitter, and tragic. This change may have been caused by some sadness in the writer's life (one of his twins died in 1596). Shakespeare, however, was not the only writer whose works at this time were very serious. The whole of England was facing a crisis. Queen Elizabeth I was growing old. She was greatly loved, and the people were sad to think she must soon die; they were also afraid, for the queen had never married, and so there was no child to succeed her.

When James I came to the throne in 1603, Shakespeare continued to write serious drama – the great tragedies and the plays based on Roman history (such as Julius Caesar) for which he is most famous. Finally, before he retired from the theatre, he wrote another set of comedies. These all have the same theme: they tell of happiness which is lost, and then found again.

Shakespeare returned from London to Stratford, his home town. He was rich and successful, and he owned one of the biggest houses in the town. He died in 1616. Although several of his plays were published separately, most of them (including *Twelfth Night*) were not printed until 1623, in a collection known as 'the First Folio'.

Shakespeare also wrote two long poems and a collection of sonnets. The sonnets describe two love affairs, but we do not know who the lovers were. Although there are many public documents concerned with his career as a writer and a businessman, Shakespeare has hidden his personal life from us. A 19th-century poet, Matthew Arnold, addressed Shakespeare in a poem, and wrote 'We ask and ask – Thou smilest, and art still'.

Approximate Dates of Composition of Shakespeare's Works

Period	Comedies	History plays	Tragedies	Poems
I	Comedy of Errors	Henry VI, part 1	Titus Andronicus	
	Taming of the Shrew	Henry VI, part 2		
1594	Two Gentlemen of Verona	Henry VI, part 3		
		Richard III		Venus and Adonis
	Love's Labour's Lost	King John		Rape of Lucrece
II	Midsummer Night's Dream	Richard II	Romeo and Juliet	Sonnets
	Merchant of Venice	Henry IV, part 1		
1599	Merry Wives of Windsor	Henry IV, part 2		
	Much Ado About Nothing			
	As You Like It	Henry V		
III	Twelfth Night		Julius Caesar	
	Troilus and Cressida		Hamlet	
1608	Measure for Measure		Othello	
	All's Well That Ends Well		Timon of Athens	
			King Lear	
			Macbeth	
			Antony and Cleopatra	
			Coriolanus	
IV	Pericles			
	Cymbeline			
1613	The Winter's Tale			
	The Tempest	Henry VIII		

Introductory essays

Shakespeare's sources

Source, Text, and Date

The immediate source for Shakespeare's play is a prose narrative, 'The Tale of Apolonius and Silla', which was told by Barnabe Riche in *Riche his Farewell to Militarie Profession* (1581). Riche tells how Silla loved Duke Apolonius, 'a very young man' whom she had met at her father's house in Cyprus. He was a soldier, however, and took no notice of the girl's attentions. Eventually he returned to his home in Constantinople. Silla followed him, but her ship was wrecked in a storm. She managed to save herself by clinging to a sea-chest, and on reaching land she disguised herself as a boy (in clothes that she found in the same chest) and went to Duke Apolonius. She offered to serve him as a page, calling herself by the name of her own brother, 'Silvio'.

'"Silvio" pleased his master so well, that above all the rest of his servants about him, he had the greatest credit, and the Duke put him most in trust' (see Act 1, Scene 4, lines 1–14).

Apolonius sent his page with love-messages to a widow, Julina, but she rejected the Duke's appeals – and instead fell in love with 'Silvio'. One day, however, the *real* Silvio came to Constantinople in search of his sister, Silla. Julina (mistaking him for the Duke's page) invited him into her house. They made love, and Julina became pregnant; but the next day Silvio left the city. Apolonius proposed marriage to Julina, but she told him of another man, 'whose wife I now remain by faithful vow and promise'. When her pregnancy became apparent, Julina named 'Silvio' as the father of her child. Apolonius threatened to kill his page, but Silla revealed herself to Julina, telling how she had left her father's house and sailed across the sea because of her love for Apolonius. On hearing this, the Duke married Silla – and as soon as her brother learned what had happened, he came back to Constantinople and wedded Julina.

This story did not originate with Barnabe Riche. He found it, in a slightly different form, in a collection of tales[1] by a French writer, Belleforest; and Belleforest made his version from the story told by an Italian writer, Bandello[2]. The ultimate source for these narratives is an anonymous Italian play, *Gl'Ingannati* (*The Deceived Ones*), which was performed in 1531 and published at Venice in 1537.

---

[1] *Histoires Tragiques*, Part IV, No. 59 (1570).
[2] *Novelle*, Part II, No. 36 (1554).

Twelfth Night must have been written at some time between 1599 and 1602. Evidence for the earlier date comes from a topical allusion in Act 3, Scene 2, where Malvolio's smiling face is said to be creased into 'more lines than is in the new map with the augmentation of the Indies' (lines 63–64). The new map in question was first published in 1599. Another clue might be provided by the name Orsino: Don Virginio Orsino, Duke of Bracciano, was a visitor at the court of Queen Elizabeth in the winter of 1600–1. And in 1602 a performance, unlikely to have been the first, was witnessed by John Manningham at a feast in the Middle Temple, and recorded in his *Diary*.

Manningham also recounts an anecdote concerning Queen Elizabeth and one of her relatives, Dr Bullein, which throws light on Fabian's cryptic comment, 'This is to give a dog, and in recompense desire my dog again' (Act 5, Scene 1, line 5). Dr Bullein was very fond of his dog, and the Queen requested him to grant her one desire – promising to give him in return whatever it was that he wanted. When Queen Elizabeth demanded the dog, Dr Bullein gave it to her and asked Her Majesty to fulfil her part of the bargain. 'I will,' agreed the Queen. 'Then I pray you, give me my dog again.'

For the present edition I have used the text established in 1975 for the Arden Shakespeare by J. M. Lothian and T. W. Craik.

The *Twelfth Night*

About the Play

'Twelfth Night' is a name commonly given to the Christian Feast of the Epiphany, which is celebrated on the sixth of January (twelve days after Christmas Day) and which commemorates the coming of the Magi – the three wise men – to the stable in Bethlehem where Christ was born. They brought with them the gifts of gold, frankincense, and myrrh, which were appropriate for an infant king.

Winter festivals

Almost all societies and cultures find it necessary to have some kind of holiday in the middle of winter. The ancient Romans used to hold an annual 'Saturnalia' for about a week in the middle of December. During this period all forms of public order were suspended: the law courts and schools were closed, trading ceased, no criminals were executed, and riotous merry-making was unrestrained. The medieval church throughout Europe adopted this festival, transferring it to the days immediately following Christmas Day (26, 27, and 28 December); on such an occasion, known as the 'Feast of Fools', the clergy in the cathedral towns would elect a boy chorister to be their 'king' for the day, while they feasted and made mockery of those things that they normally held sacred. In England this celebration ceased with the Reformation in the 16th century and its place was taken – so far as Queen Elizabeth and her court were concerned – by the 'Twelfth Night' festivities on 6 January.

15

Twelfth Night

An Elizabethan entertainment

The regular programme of events began in the morning when the Queen, accompanied by the entire court and her guests, attended chapel and she made a token offering of the Epiphany gifts. The religious ritual was followed by a sumptuous banquet. Then there was the entertainment.

It has been suggested that Shakespeare's play *Twelfth Night* was intended as such an entertainment,[1] and certainly anyone who has experienced Christmas television programmes will agree that all the proper amusement for a festive season is to be found in this comedy. It is, above all, *funny*. The humour is not all of the same kind: it ranges from the farce of Sir Andrew's near-duel to the slick word-play of Feste – and it allows maybe a few tears of happiness when Viola's lonely courage is rewarded by the man she loves. There is romance, in the story of Olivia as well as in the success of Viola – and even Maria has her triumph with Sir Toby. There are songs – old and new, sentimental lyrics and riotous drinking-songs. And there is dancing as the two drunken knights imitate the steps of the formal Elizabethan measures.

These elements have no date: they appeal immediately to all ages. But in other aspects *Twelfth Night* is a play of its own time, and although the topical allusions can be explained in an editor's notes, the modern readers – or audiences – cannot hope to recapture the first delight of the Elizabethans when they heard, for instance, that the humourless steward Malvolio, making an unaccustomed effort to smile, was creasing his face 'into more lines than is in the new map with the augmentation of the Indies' (Act 3, Scene 2, lines 63–64). We cannot share some of their beliefs, such as the ideas that passion was produced in the liver, and that the human body is made up of the four elements, but even the 21st century is still interested in astrology and notions that the planets might have some effect on the lives and natures of men ('Were we not born under Taurus?'; Act 1, Scene 3, line 112). The play's first audiences (whether or not Her Majesty was among them) must have been persons of exceptional wit and understanding: much of the comedy comes from allusions to an intellectual culture of remarkable complexity.

Malvolio

The problem of Malvolio is also solved – or ceases to be a problem – if the play is viewed in a 'festival' context. The character is cruelly treated by his enemies when they lock him in a dark room and claim that he is insane; but the treatment seems less severe if we see Malvolio as the caricature of an unpopular public figure, Sir William Knollys, the Controller of Her Majesty's Household. The official position of such a man always makes him vulnerable to satire, and it is his official duty to take it in good part.

[1] In a very imaginative study by Leslie Hotson, *The First Night of 'Twelfth Night'* (London: 1954).

Disguise in *Twelfth Night*

During the late 16th century to the early 17th century, the time that Shakespeare wrote most of his plays, women were not allowed to act in plays. Female parts were played by young men, many of whom were so young that their voices had not deepened, nor had they grown facial hair. One can imagine that their youth also meant that they were not seasoned actors.

Throughout Shakespeare's plays one can see a recurrence of female characters who disguise themselves in order to act as men – men acting as women, disguised as men. With the inclusion of these role reversals, the playwright gave the actors a respite from acting as women. This can be seen in *The Taming of the Shrew*, believed to have been written between 1590 and 1592 (before *Twelfth Night*), in which a page is hired to play the part of Christopher Sly's wife, in order to fool the drunken tinker into thinking that he was a lord. In *Cymbeline*, written around 1608 to 1610 (after *Twelfth Night*), Imogen disguises herself as the page Fidele so that she can escape an order of murder issued by her husband.

Apart from using disguise to relieve the male actors who played female roles, Shakespeare also allowed his characters to use disguise as a means of protection, and to challenge the stereotypes of gender that existed at that time. Moreover, Shakespeare also uses disguise as a means to display his skills as a playwright, creating both atmosphere and comedy through theatricality.

The use of disguise for safety and survival

In Act 1 Scene 2, Viola and others have survived a shipwreck and escaped death. Now that they are on land, one would think that they are safe, but that is not entirely the case. Viola's twin brother is missing and she is concerned for his safety, but it is her own safety that she must look to. She faces the double jeopardy of being in a strange country (Illyria) and being a woman. Although she is a woman of means and gentle breeding, she would not be afforded the protection of the state that a woman of her standing would have received in her home country. As such, she could be mistreated or hurt by anyone in Illyria who chose to do her harm. Equally, her fortunes have been lost, and with no means of support in this foreign country she must gain employment in order to survive. Employment opportunities for women were rather limited at the time. A woman without any means of support would be reduced to menial labour, which was often difficult and paid very little. Certainly, it was not a lifestyle she was used to. Thus, Viola disguises herself as Cesario, giving her protection and the possibility of being employed in areas where females were not usually accepted. She hatches a plan, along with the captain of the shipwrecked vessel, to go and serve the Duke. She does so knowing that her actions will not only cause her to escape from harm, but also that being in the employ of the Duke would give her further protection and provide for her basic needs. As such, disguise changes her identity, which in turn changes her status in society from powerless and defenseless to empowered.

Disguise also empowers Olivia. One can understand that she is mourning because of the recent deaths of her father and brother, hence the veil and the sour countenance that she wears daily. One cannot overlook, however, that she uses these 'disguises' to ward off would-be suitors, including the Duke. When her father died she was left in her brother's care. It was believed that she was left in a vulnerable position, in need of the protection of a man. This is why she has to tolerate the presence of her overbearing cousin, Sir Toby Belch, and why it is likely that she cannot resist the advances of Orsino for much longer. The veil and her grieving countenance, therefore, provide Olivia with an excuse and give her power over aspects of her life that society would normally dictate. Note that as soon as Olivia sets eyes on Cesario, she is willing to end her period of mourning immediately. This can be interpreted as evidence of the power of love or as evidence that the veil and her grieving demeanour were simply being used for convenience.

Disguise as a challenge to gender stereotypes

In Shakespeare's *The Merchant of Venice*, written around 1598, Portia disguises herself as a lawyer, enters the court (an area dominated by men), outsmarts Shylock, who is determined to get his pound of flesh, and releases Antonio from the bond that he had made with Shylock. Additionally, during this trial, Portia's language reflects intelligence, insight and sophistication which are not often associated with women. Later the disguised Portia and her disguised maid Nerissa use their wits to trick their husbands into giving up their prized wedding rings. These acts question long-held beliefs that women are less intelligent than men and that they should be confined to certain spaces.

Similarly, in *Twelfth Night*, it is Viola who concocts the plan to shed her female clothing and seek employment as a page in the Duke's court. She carries out her job as Cesario, attendant to Orsino, so skillfully and convincingly that the Duke develops complete confidence in her, although he has only known her 'but three days' (Act 1, Scene 4, lines 2–3). As duke, Orsino has several male attendants, yet it is the only female attendant (unknown to him) who impresses him so much that he entrusts Cesario with the most important responsibility of conveying messages to the woman whom he loves and hopes to marry. Clearly, Viola is not less intelligent than the men around her, nor is she incapable of performing functions that only men were allowed to do.

Viola's intelligence (and perhaps her need to escape) can also be seen in the way she staves off Olivia's advances and so avoids a potentially complicated situation. Olivia is persistent in her pursuit of Cesario/Viola. Viola, on the other hand, knows that a marriage between her and Olivia could not occur as this would lead to a revelation of her true identity. Consequently, when Olivia professes her love in Act 3 Scene 1 and tries to get Cesario/Viola to do the same, Viola artfully dodges her and vows that s/he will never again return to Olivia's house on behalf of the Duke. The double speaking that she uses in this case to avoid being cornered by Olivia, is evidence of her wit.

Disguise as a theatrical tool

When Viola lands on Illyria and makes the decision to change her identity, she emerges as a different person. All the other characters experience Viola as Cesario. The audience is aware of who Viola truly is and witnesses the complications that arise as a result of her being in disguise. In this way, Shakespeare uses dramatic irony to captivate the audience – a useful tool in the presentation of 16th-century (and even modern) drama.

One effect of dramatic irony is the creation of suspense, as it leads to members of the audience wondering how particular situations will turn out. What will be the outcome of Olivia's love for Cesario? How will the Duke respond when he discovers that the woman he loves is in love with his trusted emissary, and that his trusted page is in fact a woman? Will Viola and Sebastian eventually re-unite? If that were to happen, what then? Undoubtedly, these questions would surface in the minds of theatre-goers and keep them riveted to the events in the play.

Shakespeare also uses disguise to create humour in *Twelfth Night*. Although a servant in Olivia's house, Malvolio thinks very highly of himself. When Maria and Sir Toby trick him into believing that Olivia is in love with him and it would please her to see him wear an outrageous costume, he willingly complies. Not only does the audience laugh at the ridiculous outfit, but humour is further generated by the fact that he believes that he is charming Olivia, when in actuality she is repulsed by his costume and behaviour and hands him over to Sir Toby to be locked up for these strange actions. Later, humour can also be seen when Feste disguises himself as Sir Topas, a priest, to torment the confined Malvolio. Once again the lofty Malvolio is brought low, this time by the antics of one of the lowest members of the society – the supposed Fool. While Malvolio pleads his case to Sir Topas, the Fool makes a fool of him, which proves to be another source of hilarity for the captivated audience.

Disguise is prevalent throughout William Shakespeare's work, and *Twelfth Night, or What You Will* is no exception. With the use of disguise the playwright allows female characters to not only change their identity but empower themselves as well. Disguise is also used in *Twelfth Night* to dispel some of the widespread views that were held at the turn of the 17th century about the capabilities of women and the roles they should occupy in European society. Finally, Shakespeare's ability to create humour, suspense and dramatic irony with the use of disguise is indicative of his superior theatrical skills. Ultimately, the inclusion of disguise in *Twelfth Night* results in the play being one of the playwright's most delightful and successful pieces of work.

Gender, class and power in *Twelfth Night*

Audiences and readers respond more readily to literary works that reflect their own lived experiences because we tend to relate favourably to characters who behave like us. When audiences and readers can connect to an issue, regardless of the era, geographical space or language, we respond positively because we feel that what is projected is authentic. Additionally, we feel that this experience is real as this could also happen to us, or that this is how we might behave in a similar situation.

Shakespeare's texts are timeless primarily because they explore, and present to us, human nature. Regardless of race, class, geographical location and era, people will always display emotions and exhibit behaviours such as love, hate, ambition, resentment, jealousy, fear, anxiety, admiration, and so on. It is this study of human nature, with its imperfections, that causes audiences to be moved to appreciate these plays, even though they were written and performed hundreds of years ago. Shakespeare had the knack of getting into the minds of people, of dredging their very souls and presenting these emotions and attitudes on stage. By using the stage as a mirror, Shakespeare has put before us life, and in so doing, has reflected emotions as raw as they are deep.

The title of the play refers to the festivity celebrated twelve days after Christmas. It evokes a spirit of merry-making, gift-giving and is very carnival-like in nature. The festivities associated with the Twelfth Night are reminiscent of masking and revelry, much like carnival in the Caribbean. Thus, on one level, the play can be viewed as a light-hearted comedy, but on the other hand, beneath this revelry and fun, there are issues for interrogation and contemplation. Therefore, apart from its amusement value, audiences can find much to chew on. Through the disguise motif for instance, issues relating to gender, class and power relationships are presented.

The celebration is a parody, an occasion to interrogate structures and systems. In this space, the ordinary person can become royalty, even for a moment. Shakespeare uses a similar space of empowerment to project the women in *Twelfth Night*. In Elizabethan times, all female roles were performed by men (usually adolescent boys). You will notice that Viola (disguised as Cesario) is described by Malvolio as 'not yet old enough for a man, nor young enough for a boy' (Act 1, Scene 5, lines 133–134).Through the portrayal of the women in *Twelfth Night* (Viola, Olivia and Maria), we will discuss gender, class and power as their actions connect the major and minor plot and impact the men in the play. Audiences can find interesting and creative ways to read and interpret the text through the portrayal of these women. Olivia is a titled woman of means, Viola seems to be of noble birth but now has to earn a living to survive in a strange country, and Maria is of the working class. When we see them first, their survival mechanisms reveal their perspectives on life. Olivia lives behind her veil, Viola dresses like a man, and Maria seems to be one of the boys. They are unmarried, and the masks they wear become the symbols of their coping mechanisms in the male-dominated Elizabethan society. It is also a society divided along class lines, and one in which people are expected to know their place.

Class and power relationships

One way to approach this play is to see it as an interrogation of class, hence the dynamics of power relationships. The cast of *Twelfth Night* may be divided into two main categories – masters and servants, those who belong to the nobility (hence those who wield power) and those who do not. This kind of social order is reminiscent of post-colonial societies, where, to some degree, the descendants of slave masters still remain the dominant class, while the descendants of slaves and indentured labourers occupy the lower classes (middle class or working class). Whereas marriage in Elizabethan times might guarantee upward social mobility, in post-colonial societies, education is the main vehicle for advancement.

Elizabethan society was divided along class lines; therefore, name, parentage and lineage were important. Classism is a dominant theme in the play. To be in the upper class or the master class, you had to meet certain criteria. When Malvolio reads the 'letter' purportedly from Olivia, these words fired in him a desire to be part of the master class: 'Some are born great, some achieve greatness, and some have greatness thrust upon 'em' (Act 2, Scene 5, lines 119–121). If we equate greatness with power, in the eyes of Malvolio, even though he might not be part of the landed gentry by birth, he could elevate his status as marriage could certainly 'thrust' him into the greatness he yearns for.

The play opens with an opulent setting, Duke Orsino's palace. The Duke is love-sick and, apparently, easily bored: 'If music be the food of love, play on, / Give me excess of it [...] Enough no more; / 'Tis not so sweet now as it was before.' He is quite privileged as he is surrounded by attendants whose main duty is to cater to his every whim. Later in the act, Olivia's utterances affirm that the Duke's attributes are in keeping with the social and cultural expectations of someone of the upper class. We learn that he is 'noble', 'of great estate', 'learn'd' and 'valiant' (Act 1, Scene 5, lines 220–222).

Both Orsino and Olivia are of the privileged class as they have attendants who see to their needs by taking care of their households and entertaining them. Olivia is described as 'a virtuous maid, the daughter of a count' (Act 1, Scene 2, line 36). In the eyes of society, she is endowed with two assets – she is morally sound and she has money. Olivia's wealth, beauty and status make her most desirable as a mate and it is significant that Orsino and Sir Andrew have openly expressed their desire to marry her. We also learn that Malvolio also has eyes for his employer.

Olivia's uncle, Sir Toby, has no qualms about encouraging Sir Andrew to court Olivia, especially since he has the means ('three thousand ducats a year'). A marriage of this nature (even though Sir Andrew is a silly, shallow and cowardly man) would preserve the status quo. And even if Sir Andrew were not Olivia's intellectual equal, Sir Toby might have felt it was his duty to see his niece marry within her class. Ironically, this social rule did not hold for him as he later married Olivia's lady-in-waiting, Maria.

In Elizabethan society, women were not regarded as equals. For the most part, they were defined and governed by men – fathers, brothers, employers, spouses. Olivia's power (managing her house, assets and servants) came by default. It can be inferred that she is the power-broker only because there is no male sibling left.

By the end of the play, Maria, Olivia's lady-in-waiting, is married to Sir Toby. She is more fortunate than Malvolio in marrying 'up' as working-class women seem to have a better chance of improving their status via marriage. In the eyes of some, Sir Toby might be a misfit in his own class since he does not care for refinement and could be described as a drunken, lecherous old man, but his title guarantees him his social standing.

Sir Toby does not seem to see Maria as an inferior. In fact, he applauds her brain, skill and creativity (and would confidently leave her to execute the plan to unseat Malvolio). He admires her bold stance in interacting with him. She is not afraid to reprimand him ('What a caterwauling do you keep here?'; Act 2, Scene 3, line 64) and neither is she afraid to hurl insults at the condescending Malvolio ('Go shake your ears'; Act 2, Scene 3, line 109).

Shakespeare's working-class women are not shackled by class and societal restrictions. They can be brassy, assertive, bawdy and brave. Language is used as a liberating tool. Not only is Maria 'one of the boys', she is also the perfect companion to Olivia and respectfully refers to her as 'my lady'. She is observant – close enough to forge her mistress' handwriting (in the letters to Malvolio) and keen enough to notice her moods. Because she is so close to Olivia, she was able to inform Sir Toby that her mistress was 'much out of quiet' since Cesario's/Viola's visit earlier that day.

Twelfth Night allows for the voices of the women to be heard. Shakespeare was skilful in giving these women some amount of power even as audiences are aware of the challenges they faced in society. Olivia's wealth provides some amount of protection (she did not have to marry to get financial security). Viola could only find protection by putting on male power (by her disguise). Maria knew that marriage was a sure way of social security, especially if she was fortunate to marry someone above her class.

What is noticeable in *Twelfth Night* is the way in which the women are empowered. They are the ones who have the power (not brawn but brain). Olivia is bold enough to go against the conventions of the day and declare her love (even though apologetic and within the constraints of decency). Her veil is her power and the symbol of security. She can retreat or reveal as is necessary. Viola is smart enough to know that a single woman is not safe in a strange country. She must put on power (men's clothing) to survive in a patriarchal society. Additionally, she uses the 'man's voice' and perspective to subtly educate Orsino about women and her love for him. Maria's brainpower dethroned Malvolio (Act 2, Scene 3, lines 117–119). She is the consummate strategist and psychologist. She is the architect/director of this 'play within the play'. Her insights about Malvolio are spot on ('a time-pleaser, an affectioned ass that cons state without book'; Act 2, Scene 3, lines 126–127). She is self-assured and cunning ('If I do not gull him into a nayword, and make him a common recreation, do not think I have wit enough to lie straight in my bed'; Act 2, Scene 3, lines 117–119).

Aspirations for power

Malvolio, though occupying the highest rung of service in Olivia's household, remains a servant. He uses his elevated status as steward to lord over his co-workers. He is condescending and disrespectful to those he considers beneath him. He also knows Olivia values his service and he is equally aware that his position as steward carries power and influence. Malvolio feeds off Olivia's power and wields it with relish. When he throws down the ring for Viola to pick up, it demonstrates his contempt for those he perceives to be socially beneath him (Act 2, Scene 2, line 13). After all, in his eyes, Viola/Cesario is a mere servant for Duke Orsino.

However, Malvolio's demeanour is quite different when he interacts with those he considers above him (even if in his heart he abhors them). To their faces, he refers to his 'betters' (Sir Toby and Sir Andrew) as 'my masters' (Act 2, Scene 3, line 76). His feelings of superiority increase when he is convinced Olivia is in love with him and, thus, he is impatient with those whom he would normally tolerate ('I am not of your element'; Act 3, Scene 4, lines 105-106).

His desire to marry his employer and thus have the power to get back at his betters (Sir Toby, for instance) is evident when he's observed daydreaming: 'to be Count Malvolio' (Act 2, Scene 5, line 29), 'sitting in my state' (Act 2, Scene 5, line 37). When, in his reverie, he recalls a servant marrying his mistress – 'The Lady of the Strachy married the yeoman of the wardrobe' (Act 2, Scene 5, lines 33–34) – he convinces himself that it is possible to marry his employer.

His 'fall' could be attributed not only to his inflated ego but also to his attraction to Olivia, whose kindness and trust he may have misinterpreted for affection.

It is Maria who is the architect of Malvolio's humiliation. She sees beyond his veneer of piety and perfection. Although Olivia acknowledges that Malvolio is 'sick of self-love' (Act 1, Scene 2, line 76), it is Maria who delves into his motive and behaviour – that he is pretentious and egotistical. He is described as 'a time-pleaser, an affectioned ass' who believes 'that all that look on him love him' (Act 2, Scene 3, lines 126–130). Maria taps into Malvolio's ambition, in essence, his aspiration for greatness. Captured in one of the letters is the tension of class relationships: 'In my stars I am above thee; but be not afraid of greatness' (Act 2, Scene 5, lines 118–119). This is supposed to be Olivia's reassurance that in matters of love, class is inconsequential.

Twelfth Night

Feste the clown

Language is power. We see this in *The Tempest* where Caliban uses language as a tool to rebel and subvert. For Feste the clown, language is essential to his survival. He appropriates its creative function through his voice (in song) and through his witty exchanges with his 'betters' and social equals. Feste's power resides in words. They become his metaphorical disguise. As the clown/fool, he has certain privileges and his utterances provide him with immunity. His status as entertainer guarantees his easy movement between the dwelling of Olivia and Orsino.

Feste's interaction with the women is quite different from Malvolio's. While he respects his employer Olivia, and she appears to be indulgent towards him, he is bold enough to be candid with her. He dexterously proves that she is a fool to continue to mourn for her brother if she believes he's in heaven. He treats Viola/Cesario as an equal (unlike Malvolio's dismissive treatment) and describes himself to her not as Olivia's fool but 'her corrupter of words' (Act 3, Scene 1, lines 29–30). With Maria, Feste is just as nimble with words and their exchanges can be quite bawdy. Feste is as comfortable with the nobility as the lower class. His linguistic flexibility is what guarantees his relevance. He has to ensure that he is able to entertain so he can earn his keep. Malvolio seems to know this and insults him by calling him a 'barren rascal' (Act 1, Scene 5, line 70), in so doing, challenging his creative potential.

Ways of reading

As with any great work of art, there are many layers of interpretation and many ways to find meaning. We encourage you to read the play, perform it and arrive at your own interpretations, because Shakespeare's texts are multi-dimensional in scope. To those who read and perform, the plays can be liberating, especially if issues resonate with their experiences. For those who see issues of power relationships being projected, they might embrace the ways in which the 'underdogs' are empowered and in which the silenced voices finally take centre stage and tell their stories.

Useful terms

Allusion   A casual or indirect reference to a person, place, thing or idea that has historical, cultural, biblical or political significance.

Aside   A speech or remark made by an actor that is heard by the audience but supposedly not heard by the other actors on stage. This device, which was common in Elizabethan drama, is rarely used by modern playwrights.

Atmosphere   The mood or feeling that is prevalent in a literary work. Writers use many devices to create mood and these include setting, dialogue, imagery and plot. Often a writer establishes a mood at the beginning of a work and then sustains this mood throughout the work.

Climax   The point of greatest interest in the play, where the action changes course and begins to resolve itself.

Comedy   A dramatic work that is intended to be humorous and light in tone. It usually ends happily with an amicable resolution of conflicts.

Conflict   The struggle between opposing forces in the plot.

Denouement   The outcome, solution or clarification of a plot. It is the point in a literary work where matters are explained and resolved.

Director   The individual who makes decisions on the creative concept and interpretation of a play. The director oversees and coordinates all the aspects involved in staging a play: acting, costume design, props, lighting and sound design. The position of director is an innovation of the late 19th century and became popular in the early 20th century. Before that it appears that this function was carried out by actors and/or the playwright.

Double entrendre   A word or expression having two meanings, especially when one of these has a suggestive or indelicate connotation.

Dramatic irony   Dramatic irony in a play occurs when the audience is aware of a significant truth or situation that the other characters in the play are not.

Dramatic significance/effect   Anything about the performance on stage that generates a response from the audience, usually because of a sensory appeal. Costume, long pauses, changes in tone and mood, scene changes, entrances and exits, utterances, and so on.

Epilogue   A piece of writing that comes at the end of a literary work. It brings closure to the play and is used as a strategy by the playwright to give us a deeper insight into the characters and tell us about life after the play.

Exit/Exeunt   When a character or characters leave/leaves the stage.

Foreshadowing   The use of hints or clues that suggest events that are to come. This device is used to build the reader's expectations and to create suspense.

Hyperbole   A deliberate exaggeration used for humorous or ironic effect.

Imagery   Descriptive language that appeals to one or more of the five senses. The use of sensory details helps the reader to imagine how things look, feel, taste, sound and smell.

Irony   The common name given to literary techniques that involve intriguing, interesting or amusing contradictions. Verbal irony involves the use of humorous or sarcastic words and expressions to suggest the opposite of their usual meaning. In dramatic irony there is a contradiction between what the character thinks and what the audience knows to be true.

Masque   This is entertainment that is added to the play so as to make it more dramatic and appealing. It involves drama, costuming, music, dance and song.

Metaphor   A comparison of one thing to another, but without the use of *as* or *like*.

Motif   An incident or idea that recurs frequently in various parts of the same work.

Personification   The representation of qualities, objects or ideas by giving them human form.

Plot   The main sequence of events in a literary work. It involves both characters and a conflict and usually begins with a problem situation or conflict. The conflict increases as the plot develops until it reaches a high point of anticipation or suspense-the turning point or *climax* (see above) which is followed by the conclusion or resolution in which the conflict is resolved.

Prop   From property; any object/item used on stage to enhance the setting or performance.

Pun   Also known as a play on words; when a word or phrase can suggest more than one meaning.

Setting   The time and place of the action of a literary work. The place may be specific (country, region, community). Details such as clothing, customs and speech arc often used in establishing setting. Time includes not only the historical period (past, present or future) but also the year, season, time of day or weather.

Simile   The comparison of one thing to another using the words *as* or *like*.

Soliloquy   A dramatic convention that permits an actor to reveal his thoughts aloud to the audience. He speaks aloud to himself and is supposedly unheard by other actors who may be on stage.

Stage directions   Notes in a play that describe how the playwright wants his work to be produced or performed. They are usually printed in italics and enclosed in parentheses. Some stage directions even describe the movements, costumes, ways of speaking and emotional states of the actors. Shakespeare himself did not write stage directions. These have been added by later editors.

Subplot   The secondary or subordinate plot in a literary work. The subplot can be carried on partially or completely independent of the main plot, but serves to enhance it.

Suspense   A feeling of excitement, anticipation and anxiety. The audience is asking, what happens next? What will be the outcome?

Symbol   An object, event, person or place used to represent something other than itself, usually abstract concepts or ideas.

Theme   The central idea developed in a literary work. It is often a message about life or human nature.

Tone   This describes the writer's attitude towards his subject and readers. The tone can be, for example, serious, sarcastic, humorous, impersonal, formal or informal.

Characters in the Play

VIOLA, (*later disguised* as Cesario)
SEBASTIAN, } *twins shipwrecked on the coast of Illyria*

CAPTAIN, Viola's *rescuer in the shipwreck*

ANTONIO, Sebastian's *friend, also a sea-captain*

ORSINO, *Duke of Illyria*

VALENTINE,
CURIO, } *Gentlemen attending on the* Duke

OLIVIA, *a countess living in Illyria*

MARIA, Olivia's *lady-in-waiting*

FESTE, Olivia's *fool*

MALVOLIO, *steward of* Olivia's *household*

FABIAN, *a member of* Olivia's *household*

SIR TOBY BELCH, Olivia's *uncle*

SIR ANDREW AGUECHEEK, Sir Toby's *friend*

A SERVANT

A PRIEST

Sailors, Attendants, Musicians, Officers

Scene: Illyria. The action moves between Orsino's court and Olivia's house

1:1

Orsino, the love-sick duke of Illyria, is pining for Olivia.

Illyria: a country on the eastern coast of the Adriatic.

These opening lines are some of Shakespeare's most famous. This scene introduces Orsino. Note the connect between love and music.

If you were directing the opening scene, what kind of music would be playing? Give an example of the music you would choose. How would you let your audience know that the setting is in a palace? What props might you consider?

3   *appetite*: love's desire for music.

4   *fall*: cadence.

5   *sweet sound*: the sound of a gentle breeze.

What are your impressions of Orsino (lines 1–15)?

---

9   *quick and fresh*: keen and hungry.

10–11   *notwithstanding ... sea*: although love's desire can hold a much as the sea.

12   *validity*: value.
     pitch: excellence.

13   *falls ... price*: is cheapened and loses its value.

14   *shapes*: imaginations.
     fancy: love.

15   *it ... fantastical*: there is nothing that is more imaginative

18   *hart*: deer; Orsino, of course, makes a pun with 'heart', connecting the imagery of love with the imagery of hunting (and the associated imagery of death).

21   *purg'd ... pestilence*: purified the air (there were frequent epidemics of infectious plague—'pestilence'—in the 16th century).

22–4   *was I ... me*: Orsino compares himself with the hunter Actaeon (in classical mythology) who was changed into stag by the goddess Diana, then chased and killed by his own hounds.

23   *fell*: savage.

26   *So ... lord*: I'm sorry to say, my lord.

28   *element*: sky.
     till ... heat: until the heat of seven summers is over.

29   *at ample view*: in full sight (i.e. without a veil).

30   *cloistress*: nun (in an enclosed order).
     veiled: veilèd.

32   *eye-offending brine*: salt tears that sting the eyes.
     season: keep fresh (as brine is used to preserve meat an vegetables).

34   *remembrance*: The word must be pronounced with fou syllables ('rememberance').

1:1   *The Duke's palace. Music.*
                 Enter **ORSINO,** *Duke of Illyria,* **CURIO,** *and* **ATTENDANTS**

ORSINO   If music be the food of love, play on,
                 Give me excess of it, that, surfeiting,
                 The appetite may sicken, and so die.
                 That strain again, it had a dying fall:
                 O, it came o'er my ear like the sweet sound   5
                 That breathes upon a bank of violets,
                 Stealing and giving odour. Enough, no more;
                 'Tis not so sweet now as it was before.
                 O spirit of love, how quick and fresh art thou,
                 That notwithstanding thy capacity   10
                 Receiveth as the sea, nought enters there,
                 Of what validity and pitch soe'er,
                 But falls into abatement and low price
                 Even in a minute! So full of shapes is fancy,
                 That it alone is high fantastical.   15

CURIO   Will you go hunt, my lord?

ORSINO   What, Curio?

CURIO   The hart.

ORSINO   Why so I do, the noblest that I have.
                 O, when mine eyes did see Olivia first,   20
                 Methought she purg'd the air of pestilence;
                 That instant was I turn'd into a hart,
                 And my desires, like fell and cruel hounds,
                 E'er since pursue me.

Enter **VALENTINE**

                                  How now? What news from her?   25

VALENTINE   So please my lord, I might not be admitted,
                 But from her handmaid do return this answer:
                 The element itself, till seven years' heat,
                 Shall not behold her face at ample view;
                 But like a cloistress she will veiled walk,   30
                 And water once a day her chamber round
                 With eye-offending brine: all this to season
                 A brother's dead love, which she would keep fresh
                 And lasting, in her sad remembrance.

35 *that fine frame*: so sensitively formed.

36 *but*: merely.

37 *shaft*: arrow; Cupid (the god of love) had two kinds of arrow: the one with the golden tip caused love, whilst the leaden arrow brought hatred.

38 *all affections else*: all other emotions.

39–41 *when ... king*: when those parts of her body that govern the emotions are all dominated by a single ruler.

42–3 *Away ... bowers*: Orsino's couplet sets a final emphasis o his romantic posturing.

Discuss how Shakespeare uses the opening scene to introduce the main characters and to introduce conflict.

Note Shakespeare's use of suspense to create interest. Who is this Olivia? Will she keep her vow? Will she ever meet Orsino? What other strategy will Orsino devise to win Olivia's love?

1:2

Viola, identical twin to brother Sebastian, escapes a shipwreck. Disguised as a boy, man, she seeks to work for Orsino.

Viola is introduced in this scene. Why might this be significant?

4 *Elysium*: heaven, the home of the blessed (in Greek mythology); Viola's grief, unlike Orsino's melancholy, is expressed with brevity and wit.

5 *Perchance*: perhaps; *and also* 'by good fortune'—as in line

---

The captain recounts the last time he saw Sebastian. Although the audience is yet to see him, what impressions can they draw from this? What two words would you use to describe Sebastian?

I saw your brother ... like Arion on the dolphin's back (11–15). Note the effect of the combination of music and the imagery of the sea in this (seaside) setting.

ORSINO	O, she that hath a heart of that fine frame	35
	To pay this debt of love but to a brother,	
	How will she love, when the rich golden shaft	
	Hath kill'd the flock of all affections else	
	That live in her; when liver, brain, and heart,	
	These sovereign thrones, are all supplied, and fill'd	40
	Her sweet perfections with one self king!	
	Away before me to sweet beds of flowers!	
	Love-thoughts lie rich when canopied with bowers.	

[Exeunt

1:2

The sea coast
Enter **VIOLA**, **A CAPTAIN**, *and* **SAILORS**

VIOLA	What country, friends, is this?	
CAPTAIN	This is Illyria, lady.	
VIOLA	And what should I do in Illyria?	
	My brother he is in Elysium.	
	Perchance he is not drown'd: what think you, sailors?	5
CAPTAIN	It is perchance that you yourself were sav'd.	

'What country, friends, is this?' (line 1)

8	*chance*: possibility.
9	*Assure yourself*: be assured.
10	*poor number*: few.
11	*driving*: drifting.
13	*the practice*: what to do.
14	*liv'd*: floated.
15	*Arion*: a Greek musician who threw himself into the sea to escape from murderous sailors and was carried to safety on the back of a dolphin.
16	*hold acquaintance*: maintain friendly contact (i.e. without sinking).
19–21	*Mine . . . him*: my own escape encourages me to hope the same for him, and your words give sanction for this.
30	*very late*: quite recently.
32	*fresh in murmur*: newly rumoured.
33	*prattle of*: gossip about.
35	*What's she*: what social rank is she.

The audience is yet to see Olivia, but what do we know about her? Create a character web.

40	*abjur'd*: renounced.
43–5	*might . . . estate is*: that my position ('estate') might not be made known to the world until the time is ripe.
46	*compass*: arrange.
47	*admit*: take notice of.
	suit: request.
49	*fair behaviour*: honest appearance.
50	*though that*: although.

VIOLA	O my poor brother! and so perchance may he be.
CAPTAIN	True, madam, and to comfort you with chance,
	Assure yourself, after our ship did split,
	When you and those poor number sav'd with you
	Hung on our driving boat, I saw your brother,
	Most provident in peril, bind himself
	(Courage and hope both teaching him the practice)
	To a strong mast that liv'd upon the sea;
	Where, like Arion on the dolphin's back,
	I saw him hold acquaintance with the waves
	So long as I could see.
VIOLA	For saying so, there's gold:
	Mine own escape unfoldeth to my hope,
	Whereto thy speech serves for authority,
	The like of him. Know'st thou this country?
CAPTAIN	Ay, madam, well, for I was bred and born
	Not three hours' travel from this very place.
VIOLA	Who governs here?
CAPTAIN	A noble duke, in nature as in name.
VIOLA	What is his name?
CAPTAIN	Orsino.
VIOLA	Orsino! I have heard my father name him.
	He was a bachelor then.
CAPTAIN	And so is now, or was so very late;
	For but a month ago I went from hence,
	And then 'twas fresh in murmur (as, you know,
	What great ones do, the less will prattle of)
	That he did seek the love of fair Olivia.
VIOLA	What's she?
CAPTAIN	A virtuous maid, the daughter of a count
	That died some twelvemonth since; then leaving her
	In the protection of his son, her brother,
	Who shortly also died; for whose dear love
	(They say) she hath abjur'd the company
	And sight of men.
VIOLA	O that I serv'd that lady,
	And might not be deliver'd to the world,
	Till I had made mine own occasion mellow,
	What my estate is.
CAPTAIN	That were hard to compass,
	Because she will admit no kind of suit,
	No, not the Duke's.
VIOLA	There is a fair behaviour in thee, Captain;
	And though that nature with a beauteous wall

Line numbers: 10, 15, 20, 25, 30, 35, 40, 45, 50

52   *will*: am prepared to.

53   *character*: appearance.

▌▎ *How does Shakespeare introduce the theme of disguise?*

55   *Conceal*: disguise.
        what I am: my real nature (i.e. as a woman).

56   *haply shall become*: may chance to suit.

59   *worth thy pains*: the Captain himself might benefit.

60   *many sorts*: i.e. instrumental as well as vocal.

61   *allow*: prove.   *worth*: suitable for.

62   *hap*: happen.

63   *shape*: adapt.   *wit*: invention.

64   *mute*: dumb servant; these, as well as eunuchs, were often employed in positions demanding secrecy.

65   *blabs*: tells tales.   *let ... see*: put out my eyes.

▌▎ *The suspense is sustained in this scene as the audience is yet to see Olivia.*

Class activity:

Create a checklist, indicating the things you would consider in re-creating this scene. List the ways in which the opening scene is different from this scene.

1:3

Sir Toby Belch (Olivia's uncle) and his friend Sir Andrew Aguecheek (whom Sir Tol has brought to court Olivia) are proving to be unwelcome guests in Olivia's rather 'sober' and structured household.

1   *What a plague*: what the devil.
        niece: This (like 'cousin' in line 4) is used loosely to indicate some degree of relationship.

3   *troth*: faith.

4   *takes ... exceptions*: objects very strongly.
        ill hours: irregular habits.

5   *let ... excepted*: let her take exception to behaviour which she has already taken exception to; Sir Toby uses a legal phrase (*exceptis excipiendis* = excepting those things whic are to be excepted).

▌▌ *Note the many puns, witticisms, and innuendoes. What are the effects of these?*

6–8   *confine ... finer*: a) I will accept no further restrictions; b) I refuse to dress more finely. Sir Toby plays with the sounds and senses of the words.

9   *an'*: if.

10   *let them ... straps*: Sir Toby's variant of a contemptuous dismissal phrase, 'hang yourself in your own garters'.

11   *quaffing*: heavy drinking.   *undo*: ruin.

Doth oft close in pollution, yet of thee
I will believe thou hast a mind that suits
With this thy fair and outward character.
I prithee (and I'll pay thee bounteously)
Conceal me what I am, and be my aid   55
For such disguise as haply shall become
The form of my intent. I'll serve this duke;
Thou shalt present me as an eunuch to him—
It may be worth thy pains—for I can sing,
And speak to him in many sorts of music,   60
That will allow me very worth his service.
What else may hap, to time I will commit;
Only shape thou thy silence to my wit.

CAPTAIN   Be you his eunuch, and your mute I'll be:
When my tongue blabs, then let mine eyes not see.   65

VIOLA   I thank thee. Lead me on.   *[Exeunt*

1:3

OLIVIA'S *house*
Enter SIR TOBY BELCH *and* MARIA

SIR TOBY   What a plague means my niece to take the death of her
brother thus? I am sure care's an enemy to life.

MARIA   By my troth, Sir Toby, you must come in earlier o' nights:
your cousin, my lady, takes great exceptions to your ill hours.

SIR TOBY   Why, let her except, before excepted.   5

MARIA   Ay, but you must confine yourself within the modest limits of
order.

SIR TOBY   Confine? I'll confine myself no finer than I am. These clothes
are good enough to drink in, and so be these boots too—an'
they be not, let them hang themselves in their own straps.   10

MARIA   That quaffing and drinking will undo you. I heard my lady
talk of it yesterday, and of a foolish knight that you brought
in one night here to be her wooer.

SIR TOBY   Who, Sir Andrew Aguecheek?

16   *tall*: brave; but Maria pretends that Sir Andrew's height is being described.
     as any's: as any man is.

18   *ducats*: Venetian gold coins worth about 23p.

19   *he'll . . . year*: use up his whole estate within a year.

19–20   *very*: true, complete.
     prodigal: wastrel.

21   *viol-de-gamboys*: bass-viol.

22   *without book*: by memory.

24   *most natural*: a) quite naturally; b) like a naturally born idiot.

25–6   *gift of a coward*: talent for cowardice.
     allay: modify.
     gust: enjoyment.

27   *gift of a grave*: be given a grave, get himself killed.

28   *substractors*: Sir Toby's tipsy coinage from 'detractors' (= those who diminish reputation).

30   *add*: Maria plays on Toby's 'subtract'.

33   *coistrel*: knave, villain.

34   *turn o'th'toe*: spin round.
     parish top: A large spinning-top, lashed with a whip, provided villagers with exercise and entertainment.

35   *Castiliano vulgo*: keep a straight face (a Castilian countenance); Sir Toby's phrase has never been properly explained.
     Agueface: Sir Toby scoffs at Sir Andrew's appearance ('a thin-faced knave'; Act 5, Scene 1, line 200).

38   *shrew*: little, mouse-like creature (a term usually describing a nagging woman).

40   *Accost*: speak to.

42   *chambermaid*: lady-in-waiting.

|| *This scene would be enjoyed by the 'penny section'. Shakespeare is a master at including all classes and tastes in his drama.*

46   *front . . . her*: approach her, get aboard her, court her, make an attack on her; Sir Toby's nautical metaphors carry sexual innuendos.

48   *undertake*: tackle.
     in this company: in front of all these people; the dramatic illusion is suspended for the momentary comic effect.

51   *An' . . . so*: if you let her leave like this.

MARIA	Aye, he.	15
SIR TOBY	He's as tall a man as any's in Illyria.	
MARIA	What's that to th' purpose?	
SIR TOBY	Why, he has three thousand ducats a year.	
MARIA	Ay, but he'll have but a year in all these ducats, he's a very fool, and a prodigal.	20
SIR TOBY	Fie that you'll say so! He plays o' th' viol-de-gamboys, and speaks three or four languages word for word without book, and hath all the good gifts of nature.	
MARIA	He hath indeed all, most natural: for besides that he's a fool, he's a great quarreller; and but that he hath the gift of a coward to allay the gust he hath in quarrelling, 'tis thought among the prudent he would quickly have the gift of a grave.	25
SIR TOBY	By this hand, they are scoundrels and substractors that say so of him. Who are they?	
MARIA	They that add, moreover, he's drunk nightly in your company.	30
SIR TOBY	With drinking healths to my niece: I'll drink to her as long as there is a passage in my throat, and drink in Illyria. He's a coward and a coistrel that will not drink to my niece till his brains turn o' th' toe, like a parish top. What, wench! *Castiliano vulgo*: for here comes Sir Andrew Agueface.	35

Enter **SIR ANDREW AGUECHEEK**

SIR ANDREW	Sir Toby Belch! How now, Sir Toby Belch?	
SIR TOBY	Sweet Sir Andrew!	
SIR ANDREW	Bless you, fair shrew.	
MARIA	And you too, sir.	
SIR TOBY	Accost, Sir Andrew, accost.	40
SIR ANDREW	What's that?	
SIR TOBY	My niece's chambermaid.	
SIR ANDREW	Good Mistress Accost, I desire better acquaintance.	
MARIA	My name is Mary, sir.	
SIR ANDREW	Good Mistress Mary Accost—	45
SIR TOBY	You mistake, knight. 'Accost' is front her, board her, woo her, assail her.	
SIR ANDREW	By my troth, I would not undertake her in this company. Is that the meaning of 'accost'?	
MARIA	Fare you well, gentlemen.	50
SIR TOBY	An' thou let part so, Sir Andrew, would thou might'st never draw sword again!	

54–66 *do you think ... barren*: The sexual overtones of this flirtatious banter need little verbal paraphrase.

54 *in hand*: to deal with.

55 *I have ... hand*: I am not holding your hand.

56 *Marry*: a mild oath (= by the Virgin Mary).

57 *thought is free*: the usual retort to the question 'Do you take me for a fool?'

58 *buttery bar*: ledge made by half-door of buttery, where drink was served.

59 *What's ... metaphor*: what do you mean by talking of a drinking hand.

60 *dry*: a) thirsty; b) impotent (a moist palm was said to indicate sexual arousal).

61–2 *I am not ... dry*: 'Fools have wit enough to keep themselves out of the rain' (proverbial).

65 *at ... ends*: a) have a ready supply of jokes; b) am holding your hand.

67 *thou lack'st ... canary*: you need a drink: 'canary' was a sweet white wine from the Canary Islands.

68 *put down*: deflated, defeated.

69–70 *put me down*: lay me down (drunk); rob me of my wits. *Methinks ... has*: sometimes I think I have no more intelligence than any ordinary Christian man.

72 *beef*: This was proverbially said to dull the brains.

73 *No question*: no doubt about it.

74 *forswear*: give it up.

76 *Pourquoi*: why.

78 *tongues*: languages; Sir Toby follows this word with a pun on 'tongs'.

79 *the arts*: education.

81 *mended*: improved.

82 *by nature*: Sir Toby makes a commonplace contrast between nature and art.

83 *becomes me*: suits me.

84 *flax*: a pale yellow fibre (making linen). *distaff*: staff on which flax is wound.

85 *housewife*: The word (pronounced 'hussif') means also 'hussy' (= prostitute)—who might infect Sir Andrew with a venereal disease causing his hair to fall out.

86 *I'll home*: I will go home.

87 *she'll none of me*: she will not be interested in me.

90 *estate*: wealth.

91 *there's life in't*: from the proverb 'While there's life there's hope.'

93 *masques*: masquerades.

SIR ANDREW	An' you part so, mistress, I would I might never draw sword again. Fair lady, do you think you have fools in hand?
MARIA	Sir, I have not you by th' hand. 55
SIR ANDREW	Marry, but you shall have, and here's my hand.
MARIA	Now, sir, thought is free. I pray you bring your hand to th' buttery bar and let it drink.
SIR ANDREW	Wherefore, sweetheart? What's your metaphor?
MARIA	It's dry, sir. 60
SIR ANDREW	Why, I think so: I am not such an ass but I can keep my hand dry. But what's your jest?
MARIA	A dry jest, sir.
SIR ANDREW	Are you full of them?
MARIA	Ay, sir, I have them at my fingers' ends: marry, now I let go 65 your hand, I am barren. [*Exit* Maria
SIR TOBY	O knight, thou lack'st a cup of canary: when did I see thee so put down?
SIR ANDREW	Never in your life, I think, unless you see canary put me down. Methinks sometimes I have no more wit than a 70 Christian or an ordinary man has: but I am a great eater of beef, and I believe that does harm to my wit.
SIR TOBY	No question.
SIR ANDREW	An' I thought that, I'd forswear it. I'll ride home tomorrow, Sir Toby. 75
SIR TOBy	*Pourquoi*, my dear knight?
SIR ANDREW	What is '*pourquoi*'? Do, or not do? I would I had bestowed that time in the tongues that I have in fencing, dancing, and bear-baiting. O, had I but followed the arts!
SIR TOBY	Then hadst thou had an excellent head of hair. 80
SIR ANDREW	Why, would that have mended my hair?
SIR TOBY	Past question, for thou seest it will not curl by nature.
SIR ANDREW	But it becomes me well enough, does't not?
SIR TOBY	Excellent, it hangs like flax on a distaff; and I hope to see a housewife take thee between her legs, and spin it off. 85
SIR ANDREW	Faith, I'll home tomorrow, Sir Toby; your niece will not be seen, or if she be, it's four to one she'll none of me: the Count himself here hard by woos her.
SIR TOBY	She'll none o' th' Count; she'll not match above her degree, neither in estate, years, nor wit: I have heard her swear't. 90 Tut, there's life in't, man.
SIR ANDREW	I'll stay a month longer. I am a fellow o' th' strangest mind i' th' world: I delight in masques and revels sometimes altogether.

94   *kickshawses*: little trifles (from French quelquechose).

95–6   *under... betters*: as long as they are not better than I am—i.e. my social superiors.
     old: more experienced.

97   *What is thy excellence*: how good are you.
     galliard: a lively dance with five steps, of which the fifth was a little leap in the air.

98   *cut a caper*: jump about a bit; 'capers' are also little peppery berries served with mutton.

99   *mutton*: a slang term for 'prostitute'.

100   *back-trick*: backward steps in dancing—with obvious sexual innuendo.

> *This scene is mainly in prose, suggesting perhaps the comic purpose and change of tone.*

The Zodiac

103   *curtain*: Curtains were used to protect pictures from dust and sunlight.

103–4   *Mistress Mall*: This may be an allusion to Mary Fitton, who was the subject of some court scandal.

105   *coranto*: fast, skipping dance.
     jig: lively, jumping dance.

106   *make water*: urinate.
     sink-a-pace: another five-step dance (*cinque pace*)—with a pun on 'sink' = sewer.

107   *virtues*: abilities.

108–9   *formed... galliard*: created (and ordained) by the stars for dancing.

110   *does... well*: looks well enough.

110–11   *dun-coloured stock*: dark brown stocking.

112   *Taurus*: the Bull; the signs of the zodiac were believed to govern different areas of the body, but astrologers differed in their assignments.

Class activity:

What role do the 'minor' characters play?

i. Create a character sketch of Maria, Sir Toby and Sir Andrew.

ii. Track and trace these characters as you study the remaining scenes. Note their actions, note what is said about them and how these actions or impressions influence the play.

SIR TOBY	Art thou good at these kickshawses, knight?
SIR ANDREW	As any man in Illyria, whatsoever he be, under the degree of **95** my betters; and yet I will not compare with an old man.
SIR TOBY	What is thy excellence in a galliard, knight?
SIR ANDREW	Faith, I can cut a caper.
SIR TOBY	And I can cut the mutton to't.
SIR ANDREW	And I think I have the back-trick simply as strong as any man **100** in Illyria.
SIR TOBY	Wherefore are these things hid? Wherefore have these gifts a curtain before 'em? Are they like to take dust, like Mistress Mall's picture? Why dost thou not go to church in a galliard, and come home in a coranto? My very walk should be a jig; I **105** would not so much as make water but in a sink-a-pace. What dost thou mean? Is it a world to hide virtues in? I did think, by the excellent constitution of thy leg, it was formed under the star of a galliard.
SIR ANDREW	Ay, 'tis strong, and it does indifferent well in a dun-coloured **110** stock. Shall we set about some revels?
SIR TOBY	What shall we do else? Were we not born under Taurus?
SIR ANDREW	Taurus? That's sides and heart.
SIR TOBY	No, sir, it is legs and thighs. Let me see thee caper. Ha, higher! Ha, ha, excellent! [*Exeunt* **115**

'How now, Sir Toby Belch?' (line 36)

41

1:4

*Olivia takes a vow not to date until she has grieved her brother's death but when sh[e]
sees Viola (dressed as a man called 'Cesario') she falls in love with him/her.*

❚❙ **What is the dramatic impact of this scene?**

2–3   *but three days*: The play is operating on more than one
time scheme!

4   *humour*: temperament.
negligence: neglect of duty.

*Bear in mind the ways in which Shakespeare encourages audience
response/participation through dramatic irony. The audience knows Viola
is a woman but Orsino and the others think she is a man. Note the many
references to Cesario's/Viola's effeminate features and the dramatic effect
of 'double disguise' (Remember that in Shakespeare's time, all actors were
male). This scene introduces the theme of appearance versus reality.*

10   *On your attendance*: at your service.

11   *aloof*: aside.

13   *no . . . all*: absolutely everything.
unclasp'd: unlocked; valuable books were sometimes fitt[ed]
with locks.

15   *address thy gait*: direct your steps; Orsino's speech suits [his]
affected pose.

16   *access*: The word is stressed on the second syllable.

17   *them*: i.e. the servants at the doors.
fixed: fixèd; firmly planted.

18   *audience*: hearing, attention.

22   *leap . . . bounds*: go beyond the limits of proper behaviou[r].

23   *make . . . return*: come back empty-handed.

24   *Say I do speak*: suppose I do speak.

25   *unfold*: tell everything about.

26   *Surprise*: suddenly attack and capture (her heart).

27   *become*: suit.

28   *attend it*: listen to it.

29   *nuncio*: messenger.
aspect: appearance (the stress is on the second syllable).

32   *belie*: misrepresent.

33   *Diana*: the virgin goddess of chastity.

34   *rubious*: ruby-red; the word is Shakespeare's coinage.
pipe: piping voice.

35   *organ*: speech organ, voice.
shrill and sound: high-pitched and clear.

36   *semblative*: like (another Shakespearean coinage).
part: a) nature; b) role. Shakespeare alerts the audience [to]
the subtleties of this double disguise—a boy actor playin[g]
the part of a girl who disguises herself as a boy.

1:4

The **Duke's** *court*
Enter **Valentine** *and* **Viola** *dressed like a man*

VALENTINE	If the Duke continue these favours towards you, Cesario, you are like to be much advanced: he hath known you but three days, and already you are no stranger.
VIOLA	You either fear his humour, or my negligence, that you call in question the continuance of his love. Is he inconstant, sir, 5 in his favours?
VALENTINE	No, believe me.

Enter **Orsino, Curio,** *and* **Attendants**

VIOLA	I thank you. Here comes the Count.
ORSINO	Who saw Cesario, ho?
VIOLA	On your attendance, my lord, here. 10
ORSINO	[*To* Curio *and* Attendants] Stand you awhile aloof. [*To* Viola] Cesario, Thou know'st no less but all: I have unclasp'd To thee the book even of my secret soul. Therefore, good youth, address thy gait unto her, 15 Be not denied access, stand at her doors, And tell them, there thy fixed foot shall grow Till thou have audience.
VIOLA	Sure, my noble lord, If she be so abandon'd to her sorrow 20 As it is spoke, she never will admit me.
ORSINO	Be clamorous, and leap all civil bounds, Rather than make unprofited return.
VIOLA	Say I do speak with her, my lord, what then?
ORSINO	O then unfold the passion of my love, 25 Surprise her with discourse of my dear faith; It shall become thee well to act my woes: She will attend it better in thy youth, Than in a nuncio's of more grave aspect.
VIOLA	I think not so, my lord. 30
ORSINO	Dear lad, believe it— For they shall yet belie thy happy years, That say thou art a man: Diana's lip Is not more smooth and rubious; thy small pipe Is as the maiden's organ, shrill and sound; 35 And all is semblative a woman's part.

37   *constellation*: personality (determined at birth by the
     position of the stars).
     right apt: absolutely right.

40   *When . . . company*: i.e. alone.

44   *a barful strife*: a struggle full of obstacles.

Explain this aside by Viola. Discuss the significance of this in terms of the conflict or plot.

Class activity:

i.   Recreate this scene. Paraphrase (use your own language) the parts.
     Decide on the costume and the props for the setting.

ii. Having produced this scene, write a short paragraph summing up the
     main events.

1:5

Malvolio and Feste are introduced. Their roles will add to the drama.

2   *in way . . . excuse*: to make excuses for you.

5   *colours*: (enemy) flags; Feste also makes a pun with 'colla
     (= hangman's noose).

6   *Make . . . good*: prove it.

8   *A . . . answer*: a less than adequate answer; Lent is the
     season for fasting.

11   *that . . . say*: you can say that with confidence (i.e. that he
     has been in trouble).

12–13 *God . . . talents*: Feste alludes to the words of the Bible
     ('unto every one that hath shall be given') and the parab
     of the talents (Matthew 25:29).

13   *talents*: natural gifts (as opposed to the acquired skills of
     professional jester).

15   *turned away*: dismissed.

17   *bear it out*: make this bearable.

19   *points*: a) matters; b) laces (tying doublet and breeches).

21   *gaskins*: pants, wide breeches.

	I know thy constellation is right apt	
	For this affair. Some four or five attend him—	
	All, if you will: for I myself am best	
	When least in company. Prosper well in this,	**40**
	And thou shalt live as freely as thy lord,	
	To call his fortunes thine.	
VIOLA	I'll do my best	
	To woo your lady. [*Aside*] Yet, a barful strife!	
	Whoe'er I woo, myself would be his wife.	[*Exeunt* **45**

1:5

OLIVIA'S *house*

Enter **MARIA** *and* **FESTE**

MARIA	Nay, either tell me where thou hast been, or I will not open my lips so wide as a bristle may enter, in way of thy excuse. My lady will hang thee for thy absence.	
FESTE	Let her hang me: he that is well hanged in this world needs to fear no colours.	5
MARIA	Make that good.	
FESTE	He shall see none to fear.	
MARIA	A good lenten answer. I can tell thee where that saying was born, of 'I fear no colours'.	
FESTE	Where, good Mistress Mary?	10
MARIA	In the wars, and that may you be bold to say in your foolery.	
FESTE	Well, God give them wisdom that have it; and those that are fools, let them use their talents.	
MARIA	Yet you will be hanged for being so long absent; or to be turned away—is not that as good as a hanging to you?	15
FESTE	Many a good hanging prevents a bad marriage and for turning away, let summer bear it out.	
MARIA	You are resolute then?	
FESTE	Not so, neither, but I am resolved on two points.	
MARIA	That if one break, the other will hold: or if both break, your gaskins fall.	20

23–4	*thou ... Illyria*: you would be as good as any woman in Illyria (to be his wife).
26	*you were best*: you would be advised.
27–8	*Wit ... fooling*: Feste invokes his professional skills. *an't*: if.
29	*pass for*: be mistaken for.
30	*Quinapalus*: Feste invents a scholarly-sounding authority.
34	*Go to*: get away. *dry*: a) boring; b) caustic; c) thirsty. *I'll ... you*: I don't want to hear any more from you.
35	*dishonest*: dishonourable (for being away so long).
36	*madonna*: my lady.
38	*mend*: a) amend; b) repair.
39	*botcher*: mender of old clothes.
42–3	*syllogism*: argument. *so*: that's all right.
43–4	*what remedy*: what can you do about it. *As ... flower*: Feste's apparently meaningless chatter perhaps suggests that 'calamity' must improve and the flower will fade.
47	*Misprision*: error, misunderstanding. *in ... degree*: of the very worst kind (a legal term).
47–8	*cucullus ... monachum*: 'The hood makes not the monk' (proverbial). *motley*: multi-coloured fool's costume.
51	*Dexteriously*: dexterously (= skilfully); an Elizabethan form.
53–4	*catechize*: ask you some questions (a technique of religious instruction). *Good ... virtue*: my dear, virtuous little creature.
55	*idleness*: amusement. *bide*: wait for.

Discuss the use of humour in this scene. Show how Feste 'unseats' Olivia and demolishes her argument about grieving.

FESTE	Apt, in good faith, very apt. Well, go thy way: if Sir Toby would leave drinking, thou wert as witty a piece of Eve's flesh as any in Illyria.
MARIA	Peace, you rogue, no more o' that. Here comes my lady: make **25** your excuse wisely, you were best. *[Exit*

Enter **OLIVIA,** *with* **MALVOLIO** *and* **ATTENDANTS**

FESTE	Wit, an't be thy will, put me into good fooling! Those wits that think they have thee, do very oft prove fools: and I that am sure I lack thee, may pass for a wise man. For what says Quinapalus? 'Better a witty fool than a foolish wit.' God bless **30** thee, lady!
OLIVIA	Take the fool away.
FESTE	Do you not hear, fellows? Take away the lady.
OLIVIA	Go to, y'are a dry fool: I'll no more of you. Besides, you grow dishonest. **35**
FESTE	Two faults, madonna, that drink and good counsel will amend: for give the dry fool drink, then is the fool not dry; bid the dishonest man mend himself, if he mend, he is no longer dishonest; if he cannot, let the botcher mend him. Anything that's mended is but patched: virtue that **40** transgresses is but patched with sin, and sin that amends is but patched with virtue. If that this simple syllogism will serve, so: if it will not, what remedy? As there is no true cuckold but calamity, so beauty's a flower. The lady bade take away the fool, therefore I say again, take her away. **45**
OLIVIA	Sir, I bade them take away you.
FESTE	Misprision in the highest degree! Lady, *cucullus non facit monachum*: that's as much to say, as I wear not motley in my brain. Good madonna, give me leave to prove you a fool.
OLIVIA	Can you do it? **50**
FESTE	Dexteriously, good madonna.
OLIVIA	Make your proof.
FESTE	I must catechize you for it, madonna. Good my mouse of virtue, answer me.
OLIVIA	Well sir, for want of other idleness, I'll bide your proof. **55**
FESTE	Good madonna, why mourn'st thou?
OLIVIA	Good fool, for my brother's death.
FESTE	I think his soul is in hell, madonna.
OLIVIA	I know his soul is in heaven, fool.
FESTE	The more fool, madonna, to mourn for your brother's soul, **60** being in heaven. Take away the fool, gentlemen.

62   *mend*: improve (in his fooling).

64   *ever*: always.

66–8   *will . . . fool*: will swear freely that I am not clever (like a fox) but he couldn't even be bribed to say that you are not a fool.

Show how Shakespeare uses Feste to comment on issues such as marriage, love, traditions, madness and drunkenness. Comment on the effect of a 'fool' who appears to be so insightful and knowledgeable about human nature.

---

70   *barren*: uninspired.

71   *put down*: defeated.

71–2   *an ordinary . . . stone*: A natural idiot called Stone was a popular tavern ('ordinary') entertainer.

72–3   *out of his guard*: defenceless (a fencing term).
minister occasion: offer opportunity (for a joke).

74–5   *gagged*: unable to say anything.
protest: declare.
crow so: laugh so much.
set kind: professional.
zanies: stooges, assistants.

77–8   *distempered*: sick.
of free disposition: good natured.
bird-bolts: blunt arrows for shooting birds.

79–80   *deem*: consider.
allowed: licensed.
rail: abuse, scold.

82   *Mercury . . . leasing*: may Mercury (the god of deception) endow you with the art of lying.

Note how Olivia's observation of Malvolio (line 76) will feature as the plot thickens.

88   *hold him in delay*: are holding him back.

90   *madman*: like a madman.

92   *suit*: petition.

94   *old*: stale.

96–7   *as if . . . fool*: i.e. wisely; 'A wise man often has a fool for a son' (proverbial).

98   *pia mater*: brain.

OLIVIA	What think you of this fool, Malvolio, doth he not mend?
MALVOLIO	Yes, and shall do, till the pangs of death shake him. Infirmity, that decays the wise, doth ever make the better fool.
FESTE	God send you, sir, a speedy infirmity, for the better increasing your folly! Sir Toby will be sworn that I am no fox, but he will not pass his word for twopence that you are no fool.
OLIVIA	How say you to that, Malvolio?
MALVOLIO	I marvel your ladyship takes delight in such a barren rascal. I saw him put down the other day with an ordinary fool, that has no more brain than a stone. Look you now, he's out of his guard already! Unless you laugh and minister occasion to him, he is gagged. I protest I take these wise men, that crow so at these set kind of fools, no better than the fools' zanies.
OLIVIA	O you are sick of self-love, Malvolio, and taste with a distempered appetite. To be generous, guiltless, and of free disposition, is to take those things for bird-bolts that you deem cannon-bullets. There is no slander in an allowed fool, though he do nothing but rail; nor no railing in a known discreet man, though he do nothing but reprove.
FESTE	Now Mercury endue thee with leasing, for thou speak'st well of fools!

Enter MARIA

MARIA	Madam, there is at the gate a young gentleman much desires to speak with you.
OLIVIA	From the Count Orsino, is it?
MARIA	I know not, madam: 'tis a fair young man, and well attended.
OLIVIA	Who of my people hold him in delay?
MARIA	Sir Toby, madam, your kinsman.
OLIVIA	Fetch him off, I pray you: he speaks nothing but madman. Fie on him! [*Exit* Maria
	Go you, Malvolio. If it be a suit from the Count, I am sick, or not at home. What you will, to dismiss it. [*Exit* Malvolio
	Now you see, sir, how your fooling grows old, and people dislike it.
FESTE	Thou hast spoke for us, madonna, as if thy eldest son should be a fool: whose skull Jove cram with brains! For here he comes, one of thy kin has a most weak *pia mater*.

Enter SIR TOBY

OLIVIA	By mine honour, half drunk. What is he at the gate, cousin?
SIR TOBY	A gentleman.

102–3	*pickle-herring*: Sir Toby tries to hide his drunkenness. *sot*: fool; drunkard.
105	*lethargy*: drunken stupor—but Sir Toby wilfully mishears
108	*an*: if. *give me faith*: i.e. as protection from the devil; theologian debated whether man achieved salvation through faith or good works.
109	*it's all one*: it doesn't matter.
111–12	*draught*: drink. *above heat*: beyond normal body temperature. *mads*: makes him mad.
114	*crowner*: coroner. *sit o' my coz*: hold an inquest on my kinsman.
119–20	*takes ... much*: he says he understands that.
123	*fortified*: armed and able to resist.
125	*'Has*: he has.
126	*sheriff's post*: decorated post set (as sign of authority) before the doors of civic officials. *supporter*: prop.
129	*of mankind*: just an ordinary man.
131	*ill manner*: rude.
134	*squash*: unripe peapod ('peascod'). *codling*: unripe apple.
135	*in standing water*: at the turn of the tide.
136	*well-favoured*: attractive.
137	*shrewishly*: sharply.

OLIVIA	A gentleman? What gentleman?
SIR TOBY	'Tis a gentleman here—[*Belches*] A plague o' these pickle-herring! How now, sot?
FESTE	Good Sir Toby!
OLIVIA	Cousin, cousin, how have you come so early by this lethargy? 105
SIR TOBY	Lechery? I defy lechery. There's one at the gate.
OLIVIA	Ay, marry, what is he?
SIR TOBY	Let him be the devil an he will, I care not: give me faith, say I. Well, it's all one. [*Exit*
OLIVIA	What's a drunken man like, fool? 110
FESTE	Like a drowned man, a fool, and a madman: one draught above heat makes him a fool, the second mads him, and a third drowns him.
OLIVIA	Go thou and seek the crowner, and let him sit o' my coz: for he's in the third degree of drink—he's drowned. Go look after him. 115
FESTE	He is but mad yet, madonna, and the fool shall look to the madman. [*Exit*

Enter **MALVOLIO**

MALVOLIO	Madam, yond young fellow swears he will speak with you. I told him you were sick; he takes on him to understand so much, and therefore comes to speak with you. I told him you 120 were asleep; he seems to have a foreknowledge of that too, and therefore comes to speak with you. What is to be said to him, lady? He's fortified against any denial.
OLIVIA	Tell him, he shall not speak with me.
MALVOLIO	'Has been told so; and he says he'll stand at your door like 125 a sheriff's post, and be the supporter to a bench, but he'll speak with you.
OLIVIA	What kind o' man is he?
MALVOLIO	Why, of mankind.
OLIVIA	What manner of man? 130
MALVOLIO	Of very ill manner: he'll speak with you, will you or no.
OLIVIA	Of what personage and years is he?
MALVOLIO	Not yet old enough for a man, nor young enough for a boy: as a squash is before 'tis a peascod, or a codling when 'tis almost an apple. 'Tis with him in standing water, between 135 boy and man. He is very well-favoured, and he speaks very shrewishly. One would think his mother's milk were scarce out of him.
OLIVIA	Let him approach. Call in my gentlewoman.
MALVOLIO	Gentlewoman, my lady calls. [*Exit* 140

148   *penned*: written (i.e. composed).
       con: learn by heart.

149   *let me ... scorn*: don't laugh at me.
       comptible: sensitive.

150   *sinister usage:* unkindness, discourtesy.

152   *studied*: i.e. as an actor learns his part.

153   *modest*: reasonable.

155   *comedian*: actor.

156   *my ... heart*: my wise little sweetheart.
       by ... malice: in the face of the most cruel spite.

157   *I am ... play*: I am not what I impersonate (as the audience knows).

158   *usurp myself*: wrongfully possess my own person.

159–60   *you ... reserve*: i.e. you are acting wrongly by not giving yourself away to a husband.

160–1   *from my commission*: not in my instructions.
       I will on: I will go on.

163   *forgive you*: excuse you from.

‖ *Note how appearance versus reality is merged with dramatic irony in Viola's statement, 'I am not that I play' (line 157).*

166   *allowed your approach*: allowed you to come in.

168–9   *'tis not ... dialogue*: I am not at present in a mood to take part in such a crazy conversation.

170   *hoist sail*: prepare to leave.

171   *swabber*: cleaner of decks.
       hull: rest (with sails furled).

172   *mollification*: softener, sweetener.
       giant: Viola compares the diminutive Maria to the giant protectors who guarded the heroines of romantic fiction.
       mind: message.

174–5   *when ... fearful*: when you begin with such terrifying formality.
       office: business.

176   *overture*: declaration.

177   *taxation of homage*: demand for tribute.
       olive: olive-branch (as a sign of peace).

178   *matter*: subject matter.

Enter **MARIA**

OLIVIA	Give me my veil: come, throw it o'er my face. We'll once more hear Orsino's embassy.

Enter **VIOLA**

VIOLA	The honourable lady of the house, which is she?	
OLIVIA	Speak to me, I shall answer for her. Your will?	
VIOLA	Most radiant, exquisite, and unmatchable beauty—I pray you tell me if this be the lady of the house, for I never saw her. I would be loath to cast away my speech: for besides that it is excellently well penned, I have taken great pains to con it. Good beauties, let me sustain no scorn; I am very comptible, even to the least sinister usage.	145 150
OLIVIA	Whence came you, sir?	
VIOLA	I can say little more than I have studied, and that question's out of my part. Good gentle one, give me modest assurance if you be the lady of the house, that I may proceed in my speech.	
OLIVIA	Are you a comedian?	155
VIOLA	No, my profound heart: and yet, by the very fangs of malice, I swear, I am not that I play. Are you the lady of the house?	
OLIVIA	If I do not usurp myself, I am.	
VIOLA	Most certain, if you are she, you do usurp yourself: for what is yours to bestow is not yours to reserve. But this is from my commission. I will on with my speech in your praise, and then show you the heart of my message.	160
OLIVIA	Come to what is important in't: I forgive you the praise.	
VIOLA	Alas, I took great pains to study it, and 'tis poetical.	
OLIVIA	It is the more like to be feigned; I pray you keep it in. I heard you were saucy at my gates, and allowed your approach rather to wonder at you than to hear you. If you be mad, be gone: if you have reason, be brief: 'tis not that time of moon with me to make one in so skipping a dialogue.	165
MARIA	Will you hoist sail, sir? Here lies your way.	170
VIOLA	No, good swabber, I am to hull here a little longer. Some mollification for your giant, sweet lady! Tell me your mind, I am a messenger.	
OLIVIA	Sure you have some hideous matter to deliver, when the courtesy of it is so fearful. Speak your office.	175
VIOLA	It alone concerns your ear. I bring no overture of war, no taxation of homage; I hold the olive in my hand: my words are as full of peace, as matter.	
OLIVIA	Yet you began rudely. What are you? What would you?	

181   *entertainment*: reception.
       would: want.

182   *maidenhead*: virginity.

184–5   *we will . . . text*: Olivia and Viola employ the diction of the secular 'religion' of love.
       divinity: sacred doctrine.

187   *comfortable*: bringing spiritual consolation.

188   *text*: the subject of your discourse; Olivia 'catechizes' Viola (compare Feste, line 53).

Note the use of sea imagery in this interchange between Olivia and Viola. Why might these references be important?

191   *by the method*: according to the catechism.

192   *heresy*: false doctrine.

195   *out of*: departing from.

197   *this present*: just now; Olivia speaks as though her face were a picture.

198   *if . . . all*: i.e. if you haven't used cosmetics.

199   *in grain*: ingrained, natural.

200   *blent*: blended.

201   *cunning*: skilful.

202   *she*: woman.

203   *lead*: carry.

204   *copy*: i.e. a child.

VIOLA	The rudeness that hath appeared in me have I learned from my entertainment. What I am, and what I would, are as secret as maidenhead: to your ears, divinity; to any other's, profanation.	180
OLIVIA	Give us the place alone: we will hear this divinity.	

[*Exeunt* **MARIA** *and* **ATTENDANTS**

	Now, sir, what is your text?	185
VIOLA	Most sweet lady—	
OLIVIA	A comfortable doctrine, and much may be said of it. Where lies your text?	
VIOLA	In Orsino's bosom.	
OLIVIA	In his bosom? In what chapter of his bosom?	190
VIOLA	To answer by the method, in the first of his heart.	
OLIVIA	O, I have read it: it is heresy. Have you no more to say?	
VIOLA	Good madam, let me see your face.	
OLIVIA	Have you any commission from your lord to negotiate with my face? You are now out of your text: but we will draw the curtain and show you the picture. [*Removes her veil*] Look you, sir, such a one I was this present. Is't not well done?	195
VIOLA	Excellently done, if God did all.	
OLIVIA	'Tis in grain, sir, 'twill endure wind and weather.	
VIOLA	'Tis beauty truly blent, whose red and white Nature's own sweet and cunning hand laid on. Lady, you are the cruell'st she alive If you will lead these graces to the grave And leave the world no copy.	200

205–7	*divers schedules*: various detailed listings.
	every . . . will: every particularised item and furnishing added as a codicil to my will.
208	*indifferent*: fairly.
	lids: eyelids.
210	*praise*: appraise, make a valuation of.
212	*if . . . devil*: even if you were as proud as Lucifer (leader o the fallen angels).
214–5	*Could . . . recompens'd*: would not receive more than it deserved.
	crown'd . . . beauty: crowned the unequalled queen of beauty.
217	*fertile*: abundant.
220	*suppose him*: believe him to be.
222	*In voices well divulg'd*: well spoken of.
	free: generous.
223	*in dimension . . . nature*: in his physical form.
224	*gracious*: graceful, attractive.
226	*flame*: spirit.
227	*With . . . life*: Viola pictures Orsino as a martyr, dying for love.
231	*willow cabin*: hut of willows (the emblem of unrequited love).
232	*my soul*: i.e. Olivia.
233	*cantons*: songs.
	contemned: contemnèd; rejected.
235	*Halloo*: shout.
	reverberate: resonant.
236	*babbling . . . air*: Echo, a nymph who wasted away for love of Narcissus until nothing remained but her voice.
237	*rest*: a) remain; b) have peace of mind.
238	*Between . . . earth*: i.e. anywhere.
241	*parentage*: family.
242	*state*: present social rank.

OLIVIA	O sir, I will not be so hard-hearted: I will give out divers	205
	schedules of my beauty. It shall be inventoried, and every	
	particle and utensil labelled to my will. As *Item*: two lips	
	indifferent red; *Item*: two grey eyes, with lids to them; *Item*:	
	one neck, one chin, and so forth. Were you sent hither to	
	praise me?	210
VIOLA	I see you what you are, you are too proud:	
	But if you were the devil, you are fair.	
	My lord and master loves you: O, such love	
	Could be but recompens'd, though you were crown'd	
	The nonpareil of beauty!	215
OLIVIA	How does he love me?	
VIOLA	With adorations, fertile tears,	
	With groans that thunder love, with sighs of fire.	
OLIVIA	Your lord does know my mind, I cannot love him.	
	Yet I suppose him virtuous, know him noble,	220
	Of great estate, of fresh and stainless youth;	
	In voices well divulg'd, free, learn'd, and valiant,	
	And in dimension, and the shape of nature,	
	A gracious person: but yet I cannot love him.	
	He might have took his answer long ago.	225
VIOLA	If I did love you in my master's flame,	
	With such a suff'ring, such a deadly life,	
	In your denial I would find no sense,	
	I would not understand it.	
OLIVIA	Why, what would you?	230
VIOLA	Make me a willow cabin at your gate,	
	And call upon my soul within the house;	
	Write loyal cantons of contemned love,	
	And sing them loud even in the dead of night;	
	Halloo your name to the reverberate hills,	235
	And make the babbling gossip of the air	
	Cry out 'Olivia!' O, you should not rest	
	Between the elements of air and earth,	
	But you should pity me.	
OLIVIA	You might do much.	240
	What is your parentage?	
VIOLA	Above my fortunes, yet my state is well:	
	I am a gentleman.	
OLIVIA	Get you to your lord:	
	I cannot love him: let him send no more—	245
	Unless, perchance, you come to me again,	
	To tell me how he takes it. Fare you well.	
	I thank you for your pains, spend this for me.	

249   *fee'd post*: messenger who accepts tips.

251   *that*: whom.

258   *five-fold blazon*: a heraldic coat-of-arms five times over.
       soft: slowly.

259   *Unless . . . man*: unless the servant were the master.

Discuss Olivia's soliloquies and their dramatic effect.

---

266   *peevish*: stubborn.

267   *County*: count.

268   *Would I or not*: whether or not I wanted it.

269   *flatter with*: give encouragement to.

272   *Hie thee*: hurry.

275   *Mine . . . mind*: my eyes have had too much influence ove
       my judgement.

276   *ourselves . . . owe*: we are not our own masters.
       owe: own, possess.

As director/producer, indicate where in the script you would want the
audience to notice that Olivia is falling for Viola.

Review all the scenes in Act 1. Show how Shakespeare uses contrast to
develop characterization.

VIOLA	I am no fee'd post, lady; keep your purse.
	My master, not myself, lacks recompense. 250
	Love make his heart of flint that you shall love,
	And let your fervour like my master's be
	Plac'd in contempt. Farewell, fair cruelty. [*Exit*
OLIVIA	'What is your parentage?'
	'Above my fortunes, yet my state is well; 255
	I am a gentleman.' I'll be sworn thou art:
	Thy tongue, thy face, thy limbs, actions, and spirit
	Do give thee five-fold blazon. Not too fast: soft! soft!
	Unless the master were the man—How now?
	Even so quickly may one catch the plague? 260
	Methinks I feel this youth's perfections
	With an invisible and subtle stealth
	To creep in at mine eyes. Well, let it be.
	What ho, Malvolio!

Enter **MALVOLIO**

MALVOLIO	Here, madam, at your service. 265
OLIVIA	Run after that same peevish messenger
	The County's man. He left this ring behind him,
	Would I or not. Tell him, I'll none of it;
	Desire him not to flatter with his lord,
	Nor hold him up with hopes: I am not for him. 270
	If that the youth will come this way tomorrow,
	I'll give him reasons for't. Hie thee, Malvolio.
MALVOLIO	Madam, I will. [*Exit*
OLIVIA	I do I know not what, and fear to find
	Mine eye too great a flatterer for my mind. 275
	Fate, show thy force; ourselves we do not owe.
	What is decreed, must be: and be this so. [*Exit*

2:1

Sebastian (Viola's twin brother) is alive, and he and Antonio, the sea captain, leave for Duke Orsino's court.

1	*Nor... you*: do you not wish me to come with you.
2	*By your patience*: be patient with me.
	My stars ... me: I am an unlucky person.
3	*malignancy*: bad luck (the evil influence of his stars).
	distemper: infect.

'My stars shine darkly over me.' Why might the audience be interested in horoscopes?

Create the props you would use to stage this coastal scene.

8	*sooth*: indeed.
	determinate voyage: planned course of action.
	extravagancy: wandering around.
9	*so ... modesty*: such good manners.
10	*extort*: demand.
	keep in: keep secret.
11–12	*it charges ... myself*: courtesy insists that I should reveal myself.
13	*Roderigo*: No explanation is ever given for Sebastian's earlier use of an alias.
14	*Messaline*: a town invented by Shakespeare.
15	*in*: within.
17	*some hour*: about an hour.
18	*breach*: surf.

Discuss Antonio's role in the play.

20	*was*: who was.
22	*estimable wonder*: admiring judgement.
	overfar: too far.
23	*publish her*: describe.
25	*remembrance*: memory.
	with more: i.e. with tears.
26	*your ... entertainment*: my poor hospitality.
27	*your trouble*: for giving you such trouble.
28	*If ... me*: if you don't want to cause me to die of grief (by leaving me).
30	*recovered*: saved.
	desire: request.
31	*kindness*: emotion.
	yet: still.
32	*manners of my mother*: the behaviour of a woman.
33	*tell ... me*: betray me (by weeping).
	bound: going.

2:1

The sea coast
Enter **ANTONIO** *and* **SEBASTIAN**

ANTONIO   Will you stay no longer? Nor will you not that I go with you?

SEBASTIAN   By your patience, no. My stars shine darkly over me; the
malignancy of my fate might perhaps distemper yours,
therefore I shall crave of you your leave that I may bear my
evils alone. It were a bad recompense for your love, to lay   5
any of them on you.

ANTONIO   Let me yet know of you whither you are bound.

SEBASTIAN   No, sooth, sir: my determinate voyage is mere extravagancy.
But I perceive in you so excellent a touch of modesty, that
you will not extort from me what I am willing to keep in;   10
therefore it charges me in manners the rather to express
myself. You must know of me then, Antonio, my name
is Sebastian, which I called Roderigo; my father was that
Sebastian of Messaline whom I know you have heard of. He
left behind him myself and a sister, both born in an hour; if   15
the heavens had been pleased, would we had so ended! But
you, sir, altered that, for some hour before you took me from
the breach of the sea was my sister drowned.

ANTONIO   Alas the day!

SEBASTIAN   A lady, sir, though it was said she much resembled me, was   20
yet of many accounted beautiful. But though I could not with
such estimable wonder overfar believe that, yet thus far I will
boldly publish her: she bore a mind that envy could not but
call fair. She is drowned already, sir, with salt water, though I
seem to drown her remembrance again with more.   25

ANTONIO   Pardon me, sir, your bad entertainment.

SEBASTIAN   O good Antonio, forgive me your trouble.

ANTONIO   If you will not murder me for my love, let me be your servant.

SEBASTIAN   If you will not undo what you have done—that is, kill him
whom you have recovered—desire it not. Fare ye well at   30
once; my bosom is full of kindness, and I am yet so near the
manners of my mother that upon the least occasion more
mine eyes will tell tales of me. I am bound to the Count
Orsino's court. Farewell.   [*Exit*

> Note the dramatic significance of Sebastian going to the Duke's court as well. Orsino's palace seems to be the hub. Note the idea of intrigue and the dramatic effect that this setting will create.

> Give three reasons for the importance of this opening scene in Act 2. (Hint: the dramatic significance that Sebastian is alive.)

2:2

> *Viola realises that Olivia is in love with her (disguised as Cesario) and she herself is in love with her boss, Duke Orsino.*

0s.d.	*at several doors*: at different entrances.
1	*ev'n*: just.
2	*on . . . pace*: walking reasonably fast.
3	*but hither*: only here.

> Discuss the dramatic impact of this very brief scene. There are only two characters.

> What might be Olivia's intention in 'returning' this ring? Notice how this episode deepens the plot.

6	*desperate assurance*: certainty that there is no hope.
8	*so hardy*: so bold as to.
9	*taking of this*: response to (a) this ultimatum; (b) this ring. *Receive it so*: take the ring on this understanding.
10	*of*: from.
11	*peevishly*: rudely. *threw it*: Malvolio elaborates: Olivia simply said that he 'left it' (Act 1, Scene 5, line 267).
13	*in your eye*: in plain sight.

> 'She made good view of me' (line 17). How effective is this gesture in conveying Olivia's feelings about Cesario?

> Note what the audience is allowed to hear as Viola voices her thoughts in this soliloquy.

16	*outside*: appearance (in male attire).
17	*made good view of*: looked hard at.
19	*in starts*: brokenly, not in complete sentences.
21	*in*: through, by means of.
23	*the man*: whom she has chosen.

ANTONIO	The gentleness of all the gods go with thee!	35
	I have many enemies in Orsino's court,	
	Else would I very shortly see thee there.	
	But come what may, I do adore thee so	
	That danger shall seem sport, and I will go.	*[Exit*

2:2

A street
Enter **VIOLA** *and* **MALVOLIO**, *at several doors*

MALVOLIO Were not you ev'n now with the Countess Olivia?

VIOLA Even now, sir; on a moderate pace I have since arrived
but hither.

MALVOLIO She returns this ring to you, sir. You might have saved me my
pains, to have taken it away yourself. She adds, moreover, 5
that you should put your lord into a desperate assurance she
will none of him. And one thing more, that you be never
so hardy to come again in his affairs, unless it be to report
your lord's taking of this. Receive it so.

VIOLA She took the ring of me. I'll none of it. 10

MALVOLIO Come sir, you peevishly threw it to her; and her will is, it
should be so returned. If it be worth stooping for, there it
lies [*throws down the ring*] in your eye; or if not, be it his
that finds it. *[Exit*

VIOLA I left no ring with her: what means this lady? 15
Fortune forbid my outside have not charm'd her!
She made good view of me, indeed so much
That methought her eyes had lost her tongue,
For she did speak in starts, distractedly.
She loves me, sure; the cunning of her passion 20
Invites me in this churlish messenger.
None of my lord's ring? Why, he sent her none.
I am the man! If it be so, as 'tis,
Poor lady, she were better love a dream.
Disguise, I see thou art a wickedness 25

> *'Disguise, I see thou art a wickedness' (line 25). Notice how this idea is repeated and explored in the play. Nearly all the characters are in some kind of disguise or another (consciously or subconsciously).*

26	*pregnant*: full of ideas.
	enemy: Satan, the 'enemy of mankind' (who is always disguised).
27	*proper false*: handsome deceivers.
28	*waxen*: easily impressed.
	set their forms: imprint themselves (as a seal is imprinted on wax).
29	*the cause*: i.e. of women's susceptibility to love.
30	*such . . . be*: we are what we are made of; Viola excuses her own weakness, as well as Olivia's.
31	*fadge*: turn out.
32	*monster*: i.e. because both male and female.
	fond: dote.
34	*As . . . man*: since I am disguised as a man.
35	*desperate*: hopeless.
37	*thriftless*: wasted, unprofitable.

Create a blog in which you share your impressions of Malvolio. Be sure to mention some of what he says and does (such as tossing the ring for Cesario/Viola to pick up).

2:3

Olivia's steward, Malvolio, pays dearly for his uppity behaviour as Maria and Sir Toby play a hilarious practical joke on him.

> *Notice the use of contrast in setting and mood.*

> *This scene is long, rowdy, loud and action-filled (coming right after the soliloquy/confession which ended the previous scene).*

2	*betimes*: early.
	diluculo surgere: Sir Toby quotes part of a Latin sentence found in all 16th-century Latin grammars: *diluculo surgere saluberrimum est*—to rise early is very healthy.
3	*troth*: faith.
5	*conclusion*: reasoning.
	can: drinking vessel.
8	*the four elements*: fire, air, water, and earth; these were believed to compose all matter and, differently compounded in the human body, to give rise to four 'humours' (choler, blood, phlegm, and black bile) which determined temperament and appearance.

Wherein the pregnant enemy does much.
How easy is it for the proper false
In women's waxen hearts to set their forms!
Alas, our frailty is the cause, not we:
For such as we are made of, such we be.   30
How will this fadge? My master loves her dearly;
And I, poor monster, fond as much on him;
And she, mistaken, seems to dote on me.
What will become of this? As I am man,
My state is desperate for my master's love: 35
As I am woman (now alas the day!)
What thriftless sighs shall poor Olivia breathe?
O time, thou must untangle this, not I:
It is too hard a knot for me t'untie.   [*Exit*

2:3   **OLIVIA**'s *house*
                       Enter **SIR TOBY** *and* **SIR ANDREW**

SIR TOBY   Approach, Sir Andrew. Not to be abed after midnight, is to be
                  up betimes; and *diluculo surgere*, thou know'st—

SIR ANDREW   Nay, by my troth, I know not; but I know, to be up late, is to
                  be up late.

SIR TOBY   A false conclusion! I hate it as an unfilled can. To be up after   5
                  midnight, and to go to bed then, is early; so that to go to
                  bed after midnight is to go to bed betimes. Does not our life
                  consist of the four elements?

11	*Marian*: Maria.
12	*stoup*: jug.
14–15	*picture ... three'*: a sign-board representing two fools or asses, inscribed 'We Three'—the spectator being the third
16	*ass*: Sir Toby responds to Feste's joke. *catch*: round, part-song.
17	*breast*: singing-voice.
17–19	*I had ... has*: I would pay a lot of money ('forty' = a large, but non-specific, amount) to be able to dance and sing as well as the fool.
20–1	*Pigrogromitus ... Vapians ... Queubus*: the names are invented; Feste was obviously telling some fantastic traveller's tale.
21	*equinoctial*: equator.
22	*leman*: sweetheart.
23–5	*I did ... houses*: Feste is fooling.
23	*impeticos thy gratillity*: pocket your little tip (Feste creates his own language).
24	*whipstock*: whip-handle. *Myrmidons*: followers of the Greek warrior Achilles.
29	*testril*: sixpence. *a—*: The line ends at the margin in the Folio text, and it seems that the printer has missed some words.
30	*song ... life*: i.e. a pastoral song, preferring the life of a shepherd to court life.
33	*O mistress mine*: See The Songs in Twelfth Night, p.164.
41	*'Tis not hereafter*: it is not something for the future.
43	*still*: always.
44	*plenty*: profit, advantage.
45	*sweet and twenty*: sweet and twenty times sweet (a term of endearment).
47	*mellifluous*: honey-sweet.
48	*contagious breath*: catchy tune (with a play on 'contagious' = infectious).

Show how Feste's song reflects Sir Toby and Sir Andrew's attitudes about love.

SIR ANDREW	Faith, so they say; but I think it rather consists of eating and drinking.

10

SIR TOBY	Th'art a scholar; let us therefore eat and drink. Marian, I say! A stoup of wine!

Enter FESTE

SIR ANDREW	Here comes the fool, i' faith.
FESTE	How now, my hearts? Did you never see the picture of 'we three'?

15

SIR TOBY	Welcome, ass. Now let's have a catch.
SIR ANDREW	By my troth, the fool has an excellent breast. I had rather than forty shillings I had such a leg, and so sweet a breath to sing, as the fool has. In sooth, thou wast in very gracious fooling last night, when thou spok'st of Pigrogromitus, of the Vapians passing the equinoctial of Queubus. 'Twas very good, i' faith. I sent thee sixpence for thy leman: hadst it?

20

FESTE	I did impeticos thy gratillity: for Malvolio's nose is no whipstock, my lady has a white hand, and the Myrmidons are no bottle-ale houses.

25

SIR ANDREW	Excellent! Why, this is the best fooling, when all is done. Now a song!
SIR TOBY	Come on, there is sixpence for you. Let's have a song.
SIR ANDREW	There's a testril of me too; if one knight give a—
FESTE	Would you have a love-song, or a song of good life?

30

SIR TOBY	A love-song, a love-song!
SIR ANDREW	Ay, ay. I care not for good life.
FESTE	*O mistress mine, where are you roaming?*
	O stay and hear, your true love's coming,
	That can sing both high and low.

35

	Trip no further, pretty sweeting:
	Journeys end in lovers meeting,
	Every wise man's son doth know.
SIR ANDREW	Excellent good, i' faith.
SIR TOBY	Good, good.

40

FESTE	*What is love? 'Tis not hereafter,*
	Present mirth hath present laughter:
	What's to come is still unsure.
	In delay there lies no plenty,
	Then come kiss me, sweet and twenty,

45

	Youth's a stuff will not endure.
SIR ANDREW	A mellifluous voice, as I am a true knight.
SIR TOBY	A contagious breath.

50   *To hear by the nose*: if we hear the tune with our noses (an
     we catch the smell of breath).
     dulcet in contagion: sweet in its infection.

51   *make . . . dance*: drink until the sky ('welkin') spins round

52   *draw . . . weaver*: Music was said to draw the soul out of
     the body—but the songs sung by weavers (often Calvinist
     refugees from the Low Countries) were usually psalms.

54   *An*: if.
     dog: adept, expert.

55   *By'r lady*: by Our Lady.
     dogs: mechanical gripping devices.

56   *'Thou knave'*: In this round-song ('Hold thy peace, thou
     knave, and I prithee hold thy peace'), each of the singers
     in turn is called 'knave'.

60   *'Hold thy peace'*: be silent.

65   *called up*: sent for.

66   *out of doors*: out of the house.

Sir Andrew	Very sweet and contagious, i' faith.
Sir Toby	To hear by the nose, it is dulcet in contagion. But shall we **50** make the welkin dance indeed? Shall we rouse the night-owl in a catch that will draw three souls out of one weaver? Shall we do that?
Sir Andrew	An you love me, let's do't: I am dog at a catch.
Feste	By'r lady, sir, and some dogs will catch well. **55**
Sir Andrew	Most certain. Let our catch be 'Thou knave'.
Feste	'Hold thy peace, thou knave', knight? I shall be constrained in't to call thee knave, knight.
Sir Andrew	'Tis not the first time I have constrained one to call me knave. Begin, fool; it begins; [*sings*] 'Hold thy peace'. **60**
Feste	I shall never begin if I hold my peace.
Sir Andrew	Good, i' faith. Come, begin.

They join in the singing

Enter **Maria**

Maria	What a caterwauling do you keep here? If my lady have not called up her steward Malvolio and bid him turn you **65** out of doors, never trust me.

'What a caterwauling do you keep here?' (line 64).

67	*Cataian*: Chinese (from Cathay), villain; this is more of Sir Toby's nonsense.
	politicians: men of craft and cunning.
67–8	*Peg-a-Ramsey*: a character in a popular song.
68	*Three . . . we*: a phrase found in several Elizabethan song
69	*consanguineous*: of the same blood, related (to Olivia).
	Tilly-vally: fiddle-faddle!; an expression of impatience.
70	*There . . . Lady*: The first line of a popular ballad about Susannah and the Elders.
71	*Beshrew me*: a mild oath.
73	*natural*: naturally, like a born idiot.
74	*O' . . . December*: Shakespeare may have altered a well-known line for the special occasion of the play.

What is the significance of Malvolio's entrance at this point?

Notice that his speech begins with the idea of madness. How will this prove to be ironic later?

76–7	*wit . . . honesty*: judgement, breeding, decency.
79	*coziers*: cobblers.
79–80	*mitigation*: consideration.
	remorse of voice: lowering your voices.

SIR TOBY	My lady's a Cataian, we are politicians, Malvolio's a Peg-a-Ramsey, and [*Sings*] *Three merry men be we.* Am I not consanguineous? Am I not of her blood? Tilly-vally! 'Lady!' [*Sings*] *There dwelt a man in Babylon, Lady, Lady.*
FESTE	Beshrew me, the knight's in admirable fooling.
SIR ANDREW	Ay, he does well enough, if he be disposed, and so do I too: he does it with a better grace, but I do it more natural.
SIR TOBY	*O' the twelfth day of December—*
MARIA	For the love o' God, peace!

70

75

Enter **MALVOLIO**

MALVOLIO	My masters, are you mad? Or what are you? Have you no wit, manners, nor honesty, but to gabble like tinkers at this time of night? Do ye make an ale-house of my lady's house, that ye squeak out your coziers' catches without any mitigation or remorse of voice? Is there no respect of place, persons, nor time in you?

80

'I will drop in his way some obscure epistles of love' (line 133).

71

82   *Sneck up*: go away.

83   *round*: blunt.

85   *nothing allied*: not related.

▌▌ *Malvolio's chastising of Sir Toby and Sir Andrew is in prose. What is the impact of this?*

89–99   Sir Toby and Feste sing a song first published in 1600, adapting the words to suit their own situation.

▌▌ *What is the theme and message of Feste's song?*

> Comment on some of the puns/witticisms in this scene. Mention the dramatic impact based on audience appeal, for instance.

100   *Out o' time*: Sir Toby reverts to Malvolio's accusation of line 82.

101   *virtuous*: strictly religious and narrow-minded.

102   *cakes and ale*: festivities with eating and drinking.

103   *Saint Anne*: the mother of the Virgin Mary—an oath offensive to Puritan ears.
      ginger: used to spice the ale.

104   *rub . . . crumbs*: polish your steward's chain (his badge of office—and a reminder that he is only a servant).

109   *Go . . . ears*: a common insult, often accompanied with a gesture suggesting that the hearer has the long ears of an ass.

110   *as good . . . drink*: it would be an excellent idea (a common phrase).

111   *the field*: to a duel.

116   *out of quiet*: disturbed.

117   *let . . . him*: leave him to me.

117–8   *gull . . . nayword*: deceive him so that his name becomes synonymous with 'fool'.

118   *recreation*: source of amusement.

121   *Possess us*: tell us, let us know your idea.

122   *kind of Puritan*: i.e. morally narrow-minded, but not a member of any specific religious sect.

SIR TOBY	We did keep time, sir, in our catches. Sneck up!
MALVOLIO	Sir Toby, I must be round with you. My lady bade me tell you that, though she harbours you as her kinsman, she's nothing allied to your disorders. If you can separate yourself 85 and your misdemeanours, you are welcome to the house: if not, and it would please you to take leave of her, she is very willing to bid you farewell.
SIR TOBY	*Farewell, dear heart, since I must needs be gone.*
MARIA	Nay, good Sir Toby. 90
FESTE	*His eyes do show his days are almost done.*
MALVOLIO	Is't even so?
SIR TOBY	*But I will never die.*
FESTE	*Sir Toby, there you lie.*
MALVOLIO	This is much credit to you. 95
SIR TOBY	*Shall I bid him go?*
FESTE	*What and if you do?*
SIR TOBY	*Shall I bid him go, and spare not?*
FESTE	*O no, no, no, no, you dare not.*
SIR TOBY	Out o' time, sir? ye lie! Art any more than a steward? Dost 100 thou think, because thou art virtuous, there shall be no more cakes and ale?
FESTE	Yes, by Saint Anne, and ginger shall be hot i' th' mouth too. [*Exit*
SIR TOBY	Th'art i' th' right. Go sir, rub your chain with crumbs. A stoup of wine, Maria! 105
MALVOLIO	Mistress Mary, if you prized my lady's favour at anything more than contempt, you would not give means for this uncivil rule. She shall know of it, by this hand. [*Exit*
MARIA	Go shake your ears.
SIR ANDREW	'Twere as good a deed as to drink when a man's a-hungry, to 110 challenge him the field and then to break promise with him and make a fool of him.
SIR TOBY	Do't, knight. I'll write thee a challenge; or I'll deliver thy indignation to him by word of mouth.
MARIA	Sweet Sir Toby, be patient for tonight. Since the youth of the 115 Count's was today with my lady, she is much out of quiet. For Monsieur Malvolio, let me alone with him. If I do not gull him into a nayword, and make him a common recreation, do not think I have wit enough to lie straight in my bed. I know I can do it. 120
SIR TOBY	Possess us, possess us, tell us something of him.
MARIA	Marry sir, sometimes he is a kind of Puritan.

127	*time-pleaser*: time-server.
	affectioned: affected.
	cons . . . book: learns the rules of etiquette by heart.
133	*swarths*: swathes (literally, the amount of corn cut down with a sweep of the scythe).
	the best persuaded: having the highest opinion.
130	*grounds of faith*: belief.
133	*obscure*: ambiguously worded.
135	*expressure*: expression.
136	*feelingly personated*: fully described.
137	*a forgotten matter*: something that we have forgotten.
138	*make distinction of*: tell the difference between.
	hands: handwriting.
139	*smell a device*: begin to understand the trick.
141	*by*: from.
143	*a horse of that colour*: something of that kind (a proverbial expression).
144	*Ass*: Maria puns on 'ass' and 'as'.
147	*Sport royal*: fun fit for a king.
	physic: medicine.
149	*construction*: interpretation.
151	*Penthesilea*: queen of the warlike race of Amazons; Sir Toby teases the tiny Maria as well as praising her wit.
152	*Before me*: upon my soul.
153	*beagle*: small hound.
156	*recover*: obtain (and recoup his expenses).
	a foul way out: grievously out of pocket.
158	*cut*: gelding (a castrated horse).
160	*burn . . . sack*: heat up some white wine with sugar.

Class activity:

i. Create (or complete) a character sketch or character web of Sir Toby Belch, Sir Andrew Aguecheek, Feste and Maria. Use evidence from this and previous scenes to support your response.

ii. Dramatise the exchange between Malvolio and Sir Toby. If you were directing this scene, what hints would you give the actors? What props would you consider to portray the message?

iii. You are a reviewer from a prominent newspaper. Your jottings will be converted into a review which you will post later. Create the checklist of what you will be looking for as you watch this scene.

SIR ANDREW	O, if I thought that, I'd beat him like a dog.
SIR TOBY	What, for being a Puritan? Thy exquisite reason, dear knight?
SIR ANDREW	I have no exquisite reason for't, but I have reason good enough. 125
MARIA	The devil a Puritan that he is, or anything constantly, but a time-pleaser, an affected ass that cons state without book, and utters it by great swarths; the best persuaded of himself, so crammed (as he thinks) with excellencies, that it is his grounds of faith that all that look on him love him: and on 130 that vice in him will my revenge find notable cause to work.
SIR TOBY	What wilt thou do?
MARIA	I will drop in his way some obscure epistles of love, wherein by the colour of his beard, the shape of his leg, the manner of his gait, the expressure of his eye, forehead, and complexion, 135 he shall find himself most feelingly personated. I can write very like my lady your niece; on a forgotten matter we can hardly make distinction of our hands.
SIR TOBY	Excellent! I smell a device.
SIR ANDREW	I have't in my nose too. 140
SIR TOBY	He shall think by the letters that thou wilt drop that they come from my niece, and that she's in love with him.
MARIA	My purpose is indeed a horse of that colour.
SIR ANDREW	And your horse now would make him an ass.
MARIA	Ass, I doubt not. 145
SIR ANDREW	O, 'twill be admirable!
MARIA	Sport royal, I warrant you: I know my physic will work with him. I will plant you two, and let the fool make a third, where he shall find the letter. Observe his construction of it. For this night, to bed, and dream on the event. Farewell. [*Exit* 150
SIR TOBY	Good night, Penthesilea.
SIR ANDREW	Before me, she's a good wench.
SIR TOBY	She's a beagle, true-bred, and one that adores me—what o' that?
SIR ANDREW	I was adored once too.
SIR TOBY	Let's to bed, knight. Thou hadst need send for more money. 155
SIR ANDREW	If I cannot recover your niece, I am a foul way out.
SIR TOBY	Send for money, knight. If thou hast her not i' th' end, call me cut.
SIR ANDREW	If I do not, never trust me, take it how you will.
SIR TOBY	Come, come, I'll go burn some sack, 'tis too late to go to bed 160 now. Come, knight; come, knight. [*Exeunt*

2:4

Orsino explains the nature of love to Viola/Cesario.

0s.d. *others*: These should include musicians, as well as attendant lords.

1 *morrow*: morning.

2 *but*: only.

3 *antic*: quaint.

4 *Methought*: I thought.

5 *recollected terms*: elaborate musical phrases.

6 *paced*: pacèd.

This scene begins with Orsino requesting music (note the kind of music he likes), very much like the opening scene in the play.

List at least three ways in which this scene is different from the previous one?

16 *Unstaid*: unsure.
skittish: playful.
all motions else: all other emotions.

17 *image*: idea.

19 *the seat*: i.e. the heart.

22 *My life upon't*: I would bet my life upon it.

23 *stay'd*: looked, rested.
favour: face.

25 *by your favour*: if I may say so (with a pun on 'favour' in line 23).

27 *Of your complexion*: rather like you.

30 *still*: always.

32 *sways ... heart*: her love holds an equal balance with her husband's.

34–6 *Our ... are*: Orsino contradicts his earlier claims (lines 16–19).

34 *fancies*: loves.

35 *worn*: exhausted.

2:4

The **DUKE**'*s court*
Enter **ORSINO, VIOLA, CURIO,** *and others*

ORSINO	Give me some music. Now good morrow, friends.
	Now, good Cesario, but that piece of song,
	That old and antic song we heard last night;
	Methought it did relieve my passion much,
	More than light airs and recollected terms 5
	Of these most brisk and giddy-paced times.
	Come, but one verse.
CURIO	He is not here, so please your lordship, that should sing it.
ORSINO	Who was it?
CURIO	Feste the jester, my lord, a fool that the Lady Olivia's father 10
	took much delight in. He is about the house.
ORSINO	Seek him out, and play the tune the while.
	[*Exit* Curio. *Music plays*
	Come hither, boy. If ever thou shalt love,
	In the sweet pangs of it remember me.
	For such as I am, all true lovers are: 15
	Unstaid and skittish in all motions else
	Save in the constant image of the creature
	That is belov'd. How dost thou like this tune?
VIOLA	It gives a very echo to the seat
	Where love is thron'd. 20
ORSINO	Thou dost speak masterly.
	My life upon't, young though thou art, thine eye
	Hath stay'd upon some favour that it loves.
	Hath it not, boy?
VIOLA	A little, by your favour. 25
ORSINO	What kind of woman is't?
VIOLA	Of your complexion.
ORSINO	She is not worth thee then. What years, i' faith?
VIOLA	About your years, my lord.
ORSINO	Too old, by heaven! Let still the woman take 30
	An elder than herself; so wears she to him,
	So sways she level in her husband's heart:
	For boy, however we do praise ourselves,
	Our fancies are more giddy and unfirm,
	More longing, wavering, sooner lost and worn 35
	Than women's are.
VIOLA	I think it well, my lord.

39	*hold the bent*: stand the strain; 'bent' = the extent to which a bow can be made taut.
41	*display'd*: opened in full bloom.
43	*even*: just.
45	*Mark it*: listen to it.
46	*spinsters*: spinners.
47	*free*: carefree.
	weave . . . bones: make lace (using bobbins made of bone).
48	*Do . . . it*: often sing it.
	silly sooth: simple truth.
49	*dallies*: sports, plays.
50	*Like the old age*: as they did in the old days.
54	*Come away*: come quickly to me.
55	*cypress*: coffin of cypress wood.
56	*Fie away*: be off.
58	*stuck . . . yew*: covered over with yew leaves.
60–1	*My . . . share it*: no such constant lover ever died for love.

Show how Feste and Viola function in advancing the drama (Hint: their connection with/to Orsino and Olivia).

70	*pains*: troubles (i.e. in singing).
73	*pleasure . . . another*: Feste alludes to the proverbial notion that pleasure must be paid for with pain.
74	*Give . . . thee*: Orsino dismisses Feste with wit and courtesy.
75	*the melancholy god*: Saturn, whose planetary influence shed gloom on those born under it.
76	*doublet*: sleeveless jacket.
	changeable taffeta: iridescent silk.
	opal: a semi-precious stone which changes colour in different lights.
76–7	*I . . . sea*: I think men like you should become sea-merchants.
77–8	*that . . . everywhere*: so that they could deal in everything and trade everywhere.
78	*intent*: port of call.
78–9	*that's . . . nothing*: that's the way to make a profitable business from nothing.

ORSINO	Then let thy love be younger than thyself,
	Or thy affection cannot hold the bent.
	For women are as roses, whose fair flower 40
	Being once display'd, doth fall that very hour.
VIOLA	And so they are: alas, that they are so.
	To die, even when they to perfection grow!

Enter **CURIO** *and* **FESTE**

ORSINO	O, fellow, come, the song we had last night.
	Mark it, Cesario—it is old and plain; 45
	The spinsters and the knitters in the sun,
	And the free maids that weave their threads with bones
	Do use to chant it: it is silly sooth,
	And dallies with the innocence of love,
	Like the old age. 50
FESTE	Are you ready, sir?
ORSINO	Ay, prithee sing.
	Music
FESTE	*Come away, come away death,*
	And in sad cypress let me be laid. 55
	Fie away, fie away breath,
	I am slain by a fair cruel maid:
	My shroud of white, stuck all with yew,
	O prepare it.
	My part of death no one so true 60
	Did share it.
	Not a flower, not a flower sweet,
	On my black coffin let there be strewn:
	Not a friend, not a friend greet
	My poor corpse, where my bones shall be thrown: 65
	A thousand thousand sighs to save,
	Lay me, O where
	Sad true lover never find my grave,
	To weep there.
ORSINO	There's for thy pains. [*Gives him money*] 70
FESTE	No pains, sir, I take pleasure in singing, sir.
ORSINO	I'll pay thy pleasure then.
FESTE	Truly sir, and pleasure will be paid, one time or another.
ORSINO	Give me now leave to leave thee.
FESTE	Now the melancholy god protect thee, and the tailor make thy 75
	doublet of changeable taffeta, for thy mind is a very opal. I
	would have men of such constancy put to sea, that their business
	might be everything, and their intent everywhere, for that's it
	that always makes a good voyage of nothing. Farewell. [*Exit*

80	*give place*: take themselves away.
82	*yond*: yonder.
	sovereign cruelty: queen of cruelty.
83	*than the world*: than any other in the world.
85	*The parts*: i.e. the wealth and social status.
86	*hold*: value.
	giddily: lightly, carelessly; Fortune is fickle in her distribution of worldly goods.
87	*that ... gems*: i.e. her beauty.
88	*pranks her in*: adorns her with.
91	*Sooth*: indeed.

> What is Orsino's opinion on love? Use quotations from the play to support your response.

97	*bide*: endure.
99	*retention*: the ability to retain (a medical term).
100	*appetite*: desire, lust.
101	*No ... liver*: not an emotion arising out of the liver (thought to be the seat of love).
102	*That ... revolt*: that can be surfeited, cloyed, and revolted (by over-eating).
115	*a blank*: a blank page.
116	*concealment ... bud*: secrecy like a canker-worm destroying a budding rose from the inside.
117	*damask*: blended red and white.
	thought: sadness.
118	*with ... melancholy*: pale and sick with misery.
119–120	*like ... grief*: like the smiling figure of Patience cut on a tombstone.
122	*Our ... will*: we show greater passion than we feel.
	still: always.

| *This issue of unrequited love is hinted at.*

| *'I am all the daughters of my father's house' (line 125). Why is this significant?*

| ORSINO | Let all the rest give place. | 80 |

[Exeunt **CURIO** *and* **ATTENDANTS***

	Once more, Cesario,	
	Get thee to yond same sovereign cruelty.	
	Tell her my love, more noble than the world,	
	Prizes not quantity of dirty lands:	
	The parts that fortune hath bestow'd upon her,	85
	Tell her I hold as giddily as fortune.	
	But 'tis that miracle and queen of gems	
	That nature pranks her in, attracts my soul.	

| VIOLA | But if she cannot love you, sir? | |

| ORSINO | I cannot be so answer'd. | 90 |

VIOLA	Sooth, but you must.	
	Say that some lady—as perhaps there is—	
	Hath for your love as great a pang of heart	
	As you have for Olivia: you cannot love her;	
	You tell her so. Must she not then be answer'd?	95

ORSINO	There is no woman's sides	
	Can bide the beating of so strong a passion	
	As love doth give my heart; no woman's heart	
	So big, to hold so much. They lack retention.	
	Alas, their love may be call'd appetite,	100
	No motion of the liver, but the palate,	
	That suffers surfeit, cloyment, and revolt;	
	But mine is all as hungry as the sea,	
	And can digest as much. Make no compare	
	Between that love a woman can bear me	105
	And that I owe Olivia.	

| VIOLA | Ay, but I know— | |

| ORSINO | What dost thou know? | |

VIOLA	Too well what love women to men may owe.	
	In faith, they are as true of heart as we.	110
	My father had a daughter lov'd a man—	
	As it might be, perhaps, were I a woman,	
	I should your lordship.	

| ORSINO | And what's her history? | |

VIOLA	A blank, my lord. She never told her love,	115
	But let concealment, like a worm i' th' bud,	
	Feed on her damask cheek. She pin'd in thought,	
	And with a green and yellow melancholy	
	She sat like Patience on a monument,	
	Smiling at grief. Was not this love indeed?	120
	We men may say more, swear more, but indeed	
	Our shows are more than will: for still we prove	
	Much in our vows, but little in our love.	

127   *shall I to*: shall I go to.

128   *theme*: business.

130   *give no place*: not be held back.
       bide no denay: accept no refusal.

Class activity:

i.   Paraphrase Feste's song. Show how it introduces or reinforces a theme in the play.

ii.   Recreate the practical joke played on Malvolio. What props could be used in this scene?

iii.   Show how you could portray/dramatise the idea of eavesdropping.

iv.   Discuss how the idea of ambition is presented.

v.   What does the audience learn about Malvolio's feelings about Sir Toby?

vi.   List the contents of the letter Malvolio receives and his response to each point.

2:5

Sir Toby and his friends watch Malvolio as he reads the letter Maria has written.

0s.d.   *Fabian*: Fabian will take the place that Maria assigned to Feste (Act 2, Scene 3, line 148).

1   *Come thy ways*: come along.

2   *a scruple*: a very tiny part.
      boiled: Fabian's pronunciation ('biled') puns on the 'blac bile' that was said to cause melancholy (see Act 2, Scene line 8 note).

5   *sheep-biter*: dissembler.
      come . . . shame: be disgraced.

7   *a bear-baiting*: A popular 'sport' in which a bear, tethered to a post, was tormented by dogs.

8–9   *fool . . . blue*: bruise him with fooling.

10   *An'*: and (= if).
      it is . . . lives: we don't deserve to live.

11   *my . . . India*: my precious pure gold.

12   *box-tree*: an evergreen shrub used for garden hedges.

13–14   *practising . . . shadow*: rehearsing gestures, using his shadow as a looking glass.

14   *this half hour*: for the past half hour.

15   *contemplative*: self-deceiving.

16   *Close*: hide and keep quiet.

18   *tickling*: flattery (as poachers catch trout by tickling them

ORSINO	But died thy sister of her love, my boy?
VIOLA	I am all the daughters of my father's house, 125 And all the brothers too: and yet I know not. Sir, shall I to this lady?
ORSINO	Ay, that's the theme. To her in haste; give her this jewel; say My love can give no place, bide no denay. [*Exeunt* 130

2:5   **OLIVIA**'s *garden*
Enter **SIR TOBY, SIR ANDREW,** *and* **FABIAN**

SIR TOBY	Come thy ways, Signior Fabian.
FABIAN	Nay, I'll come. If I lose a scruple of this sport, let me be boiled to death with melancholy.
SIR TOBY	Would'st thou not be glad to have the niggardly rascally sheep-biter come by some notable shame? 5
FABIAN	I would exult, man: you know he brought me out o' favour with my lady about a bear-baiting here.
SIR TOBY	To anger him we'll have the bear again, and we will fool him black and blue—shall we not, Sir Andrew?
SIR ANDREW	An' we do not, it is pity of our lives. 10

Enter **MARIA**

SIR TOBY	Here comes the little villain. How now, my metal of India?
MARIA	Get ye all three into the box-tree. Malvolio's coming down this walk; he has been yonder i' the sun practising behaviour to his own shadow this half hour. Observe him, for the love of mockery; for I know this letter will make a contemplative 15 idiot of him. Close, in the name of jesting! [*The men hide.* Maria *drops a letter*] Lie thou there, for here comes the trout that must be caught with tickling. [*Exit*

19	*she*: i.e. Olivia.
20	*affect*: care for.
21	*fancy*: love.
	one . . . complexion: someone like me in appearance and temperament.
22	*uses*: treats.
23	*follows*: serves.
25	*Contemplation*: conceit.
26	*jets*: struts.
	advanced: outspread.
27	*'Slight*: by God's light.

▌▌ *Note the bird imagery – turkey-cock, plumes (lines 25–26); gull-catcher (line 159).*

33	*example*: precedent.
33–4	*The . . . wardrobe*: An inexplicable joke with perhaps topical significance: William Strachey was a shareholder in a rival theatre, and David Yeomans was a wardrobe-keeper for the same company.
35	*Jezebel*: the proud wife of King Ahab (2 Kings 9:30–37).
36	*blows*: swells.
37	*state*: chair of state.
38	*stone-bow*: crossbow which fired stones.
39	*branched*: embroidered (with a design of tree-branches).
40	*day-bed*: couch.
43	*to have . . . state*: to adopt the grand manner.
43–4	*demure . . . regard*: serious look around at those present.
45	*my kinsman Toby*: Malvolio speaks with familiarity, neglecting to say 'Sir Toby'.
46	*Bolts and shackles*: fetters.
48	*with . . . start*: jumping obediently to attention.
	make out for: go off to find.
49	*the while*: during the meantime.
50	*my . . . jewel*: Malvolio suddenly remembers that in his new role he will not wear the steward's chain of office.
51	*curtsies*: bows down low.
53	*with cars*: with chariots, by force.
55	*austere . . . control*: stern look of authority.
56	*take*: give.

Enter **MALVOLIO**

MALVOLIO	'Tis but fortune, all is fortune. Maria once told me she did affect me, and I have heard herself come thus near,	20
	that should she fancy, it should be one of my complexion. Besides, she uses me with a more exalted respect than any one else that follows her. What should I think on't?	
SIR TOBY	Here's an overweening rogue!	
FABIAN	O, peace! Contemplation makes a rare turkey-cock of him: how he jets under his advanced plumes!	25
SIR ANDREW	'Slight, I could so beat the rogue!	
SIR TOBY	Peace, I say!	
MALVOLIO	To be Count Malvolio!	
SIR TOBY	Ah, rogue!	30
SIR ANDREW	Pistol him, pistol him!	
SIR TOBY	Peace, peace!	
MALVOLIO	There is example for't. The Lady of the Strachy married the yeoman of the wardrobe.	
SIR ANDREW	Fie on him, Jezebel!	35
FABIAN	O peace! Now he's deeply in. Look how imagination blows him.	
MALVOLIO	Having been three months married to her, sitting in my state—	
SIR TOBY	O for a stone-bow to hit him in the eye!	
MALVOLIO	Calling my officers about me, in my branched velvet gown, having come from a day-bed, where I have left Olivia sleeping—	40
SIR TOBY	Fire and brimstone!	
FABIAN	O peace, peace!	
MALVOLIO	And then to have the humour of state; and after a demure travel of regard, telling them I know my place, as I would they should do theirs, to ask for my kinsman Toby.	45
SIR TOBY	Bolts and shackles!	
FABIAN	O peace, peace, peace! Now, now!	
MALVOLIO	Seven of my people with an obedient start make out for him. I frown the while, and perchance wind up my watch, or play with my [*Touching his chain*]—some rich jewel. Toby approaches; curtsies there to me—	50
SIR TOBY	Shall this fellow live?	
FABIAN	Though our silence be drawn from us with cars, yet peace!	
MALVOLIO	I extend my hand to him thus, quenching my familiar smile with a austere regard of control—	55
SIR TOBY	And does not Toby take you a blow o' the lips then?	

61	*scab*: a term of abuse.
62	*break the sinews*: cut the hamstrings, disable.
63	*treasure of your time*: your valuable time.
68	*employment*: business.
69	*woodcock*: a proverbially foolish bird. *gin*: trap, snare.
70–1	*the spirit ... him*: may some whimsical impulse inspire him to read it aloud.
72	*hand*: handwriting.
73	*her ... T's*: Malvolio spells out a slang word for the female genitalia.
73–4	*makes ... P's*: i.e. urinates; the joke is unmistakable when the words are spoken.
74	*in ... question*: beyond all doubt.
77	*Soft*: gently.
78	*impressure ... seal*: the picture of Lucrece which she usually stamps on her letters. *Lucrece*: a Roman matron who committed suicide when she was violated by Tarquin; her story is told in Shakespeare's narrative poem *The Rape of Lucrece*.
81	*liver and all*: to the heart of his passion.
86	*numbers*: versification.
88	*brock*: badger (noted for its foul smell).
90	*Lucrece knife*: knife that Lucrece killed herself with.
93	*fustian*: ridiculous.
94	*wench*: i.e. Maria.

MALVOLIO	Saying, 'Cousin Toby, my fortunes having cast me on your niece give me this prerogative of speech'.
SIR TOBY	What, what?
MALVOLIO	'You must amend your drunkenness.' 60
SIR TOBY	Out, scab!
FABIAN	Nay, patience, or we break the sinews of our plot.
MALVOLIO	'Besides, you waste the treasure of your time with a foolish knight.'
SIR ANDREW	That's me, I warrant you. 65
MALVOLIO	'One Sir Andrew.'
SIR ANDREW	I knew 'twas I, for many do call me fool.
MALVOLIO	[*Seeing the letter*] What employment have we here?
FABIAN	Now is the woodcock near the gin.
SIR TOBY	O peace! And the spirit of humours intimate reading aloud to him! 70
MALVOLIO	[*Picking up the letter*] By my life, this is my lady's hand: these be her very C's, her U's, and her T's, and thus makes she her great P's. It is in contempt of question her hand.
SIR ANDREW	Her C's, her U's, and her T's: why that? 75
MALVOLIO	[*Reads*] *To the unknown beloved, this, and my good wishes.* Her very phrases! By your leave, wax. Soft! and the impressure her Lucrece, with which she uses to seal. 'Tis my lady! To whom should this be?
	He opens the letter 80
FABIAN	This wins him, liver and all.

MALVOLIO	[*Reads*] *Jove knows I love;*
	                     But who?
	                     Lips, do not move,
	                     No man must know. 85
	'No man must know'! What follows? The numbers altered! 'No man must know'! If this should be thee, Malvolio!

SIR TOBY	Marry, hang thee, brock!

MALVOLIO	[*Reads*] *I may command where I adore;*
	                     But silence, like a Lucrece knife, 90
	                     With bloodless stroke my heart doth gore;
	                     M.O.A.I. doth sway my life.

FABIAN	A fustian riddle!
SIR TOBY	Excellent wench, say I.
MALVOLIO	'M.O.A.I. doth sway my life.'—Nay, but first let me see, let me see, let me see. 95

97   *dressed*: prepared for.

98   *with . . . at it*: just see how the bird is led astray by it.
staniel: an inferior kind of hawk.

101   *formal capacity*: reasonable mind.
obstruction: problem.

102   *position*: arrangement.

104   *O ay*: Sir Toby repeats Malvolio's 'O.A.'
make up: complete.
at . . . scent: without a clue.

105   *Sowter . . . fox*: although it stinks like a fox, that old hound will give tongue to it.

107   *cur*: worthless dog.
excellent at faults: good at picking up cold scents.

108–9   *no . . . probation*: no consistency in what follows that will hold up under examination.

110   *'O' shall end*: he will cry 'O' in shame.

111   *cudgel*: beat.

112   *behind*: at the end.

114   *detraction . . . heels*: bad luck following you.

115   *simulation*: puzzle (disguised letters).

116   *crush*: force.
bow: point.

118   *revolve*: reflect, consider.
stars: fortune.

FABIAN	What dish o' poison has she dressed him!
SIR TOBY	And with what wing the staniel checks at it!
MALVOLIO	'I may command where I adore.' Why, she may command me: I serve her, she is my lady. Why, this is evident to any **100** formal capacity. There is no obstruction in this. And the end: what should that alphabetical position portend? If I could make that resemble something in me! Softly! 'M.O.A.I.'—
SIR TOBY	O ay, make up that! He is now at a cold scent.
FABIAN	Sowter will cry upon't for all this, though it be as rank as a fox. **105**
MALVOLIO	'M'—Malvolio! 'M'! Why, that begins my name!
FABIAN	Did not I say he would work it out? the cur is excellent at faults.
MALVOLIO	'M'—But then there is no consonancy in the sequel; that suffers under probation: 'A' should follow, but 'O' does.
FABIAN	And 'O' shall end, I hope. **110**
SIR TOBY	Ay, or I'll cudgel him, and make him cry 'O'!
MALVOLIO	And then 'I' comes behind.
FABIAN	Ay, an' you had any eye behind you, you might see more detraction at your heels than fortunes before you.
MALVOLIO	'M.O.A.I.' This simulation is not as the former: and yet, to **115** crush this a little, it would bow to me, for every one of these letters are in my name. Soft! Here follows prose. [*Reads*]

> *If this fall into thy hand, revolve. In my stars I am*
> *above thee, but be not afraid of greatness. Some*
> *are born great, some achieve greatness, and some*   **120**

Malvolio intrigued by the letter.

121–2	*open their hands*: make a generous offer.
122	*blood and spirit*: spirited courage.
123	*inure*: accustom. *like*: likely.
123–4	*cast . . . slough*: throw off your humility as a snake sloughs off its old skin.
124	*opposite*: disagreeable.
126	*tang . . . state*: speak out on important subjects. *trick*: affectation.
127	*singularity*: eccentricity.
129	*ever*: always. *cross-gartered*: garters crossing round the leg and fastening in a bow above the knee (see illustration p.55).
130	*Go to*: come on. *thou art made*: your fortune is made.
131	*still*: always.
133	*alter services*: so that Malvolio became master (see Act 5, Scene 1, lines 337–338).
135	*champaign*: open country. *discovers*: reveals.
135–6	*open*: unmistakable. *politic authors*: political books.
136	*baffle*: treat with contempt (technically, 'baffle' = 'to degrade from knighthood').
137	*wash off*: cast off. *gross acquaintance*: any knowledge of common things or people.
138	*point-device*: precisely.
139	*jade*: deceive. *every reason excites*: every argument persuades.
140	*of late*: recently.
142	*injunction*: command.
143	*habits*: clothes.
144	*strange*: distant, aloof. *stout*: proud.
145	*even . . . on*: as quickly as I can get them on.
147–8	*thou entertain'st*: you accept.
149	*become*: suit.
150	*still*: always.
154	*the Sophy*: the Shah of Persia (who was very generous to two English brothers who visited Persia in 1599).

have greatness thrust upon 'em. Thy fates open
their hands, let thy blood and spirit embrace them;
and to inure thyself to what thou art like to be, cast
thy humble slough, and appear fresh. Be opposite
with a kinsman, surly with servants. Let thy tongue   125
tang arguments of state. Put thyself into the trick of
singularity. She thus advises thee, that sighs for thee.
Remember who commended thy yellow stockings,
and wished to see thee ever cross-gartered. I say,
remember. Go to, thou art made—if thou desir'st   130
to be so. If not, let me see thee a steward still, the
fellow of servants, and not worthy to touch Fortune's
fingers. Farewell. She that would alter services
with thee,   *The Fortunate Unhappy.*

Daylight and champaign discovers not more! This is open.   135
I will be proud, I will read politic authors, I will baffle
Sir Toby, I will wash off gross acquaintance, I will be
point-device the very man. I do not now fool myself, to let
imagination jade me; for every reason excites to this, that my
lady loves me. She did commend my yellow stockings of late,   140
she did praise my leg being cross-gartered; and in this she
manifests herself to my love, and with a kind of injunction
drives me to these habits of her liking. I thank my stars, I am
happy! I will be strange, stout, in yellow stockings, and cross-
gartered, even with the swiftness of putting on. Jove and my   145
stars be praised!—Here is yet a postscript. [*Reads*]

Thou canst not choose but know who I am. If thou
entertain'st my love, let it appear in thy smiling; thy
smiles become thee well. Therefore in my presence
still smile, dear my sweet, I prithee.   150

Jove, I thank thee! I will smile, I will do every thing that thou
wilt have me.   [*Exit*

FABIAN   I will not give my part of this sport for a pension of thousands
to be paid from the Sophy.

159 *gull-catcher*: catcher of fools.

160 *set . . . neck*: i.e. as a sign of conquest.

162 *play*: gamble.
     tray-trip: a dice-game where a player had to throw a three
     to win.

168 *aqua-vitae*: alcoholic liquor.

175 *notable contempt*: famous disgrace.

176 *Tartar*: Tartarus—hell.

177 *make one*: join the party.

Sir Toby	I could marry this wench for this device.	155
Sir Andrew	So could I too.	
Sir Toby	And ask no other dowry with her but such another jest.	

Enter **Maria**

Sir Andrew	Nor I neither.	
Fabian	Here comes my noble gull-catcher.	
Sir Toby	Wilt thou set thy foot o' my neck?	160
Sir Andrew	Or o' mine either?	
Sir Toby	Shall I play my freedom at tray-trip, and become thy bond-slave?	
Sir Andrew	I' faith, or I either?	
Sir Toby	Why, thou hast put him in such a dream, that when the image of it leaves him he must run mad.	165
Maria	Nay, but say true, does it work upon him?	
Sir Toby	Like aqua-vitae with a midwife.	
Maria	If you will then see the fruits of the sport, mark his first approach before my lady: he will come to her in yellow stockings, and 'tis a colour she abhors; and cross-gartered, a fashion she detests; and he will smile upon her, which will now be so unsuitable to her disposition, being addicted to a melancholy as she is, that it cannot but turn him into a notable contempt. If you will see it, follow me.	170 175
Sir Toby	To the gates of Tartar, thou most excellent devil of wit!	
Sir Andrew	I'll make one too. *[Exeunt*	

3:1

The disguised Viola (Cesario) meets Feste and the two knights who are staying at Olivia's house. Olivia declares her love for Cesario who is in the employ of Orsino.

0s.d.	*tabor*: small drum; pipe and tabor were traditional instruments of the stage clown.
1	*Save*: God save.
	live by: earn a living with.
3	*churchman*: priest.
4	*by*: near.
6	*lies by*: a) lies near; b) lies with.
7	*stands by*: is maintained by.
9	*You have said*: just as you say.
	To . . . age: what an age we live in.
9–10	*A sentence . . . wit*: a wise saying is like a soft glove to a clever man.
9	*chev'ril*: kidskin, a soft pliable leather.
12	*dally nicely*: play curiously.
13	*wanton*: wayward, disorderly.
14	*I . . . name*: that's why I wish my sister had no name.
17–18	*words . . . them*: words have become very untrustworthy now that verbal promises ('bonds') cannot be relied on.
20	*Troth*: by my truth.

Comment on Feste's role.

What effect do Feste's utterances have on the audience?

To what extent are these utterances in keeping with the things he says in Act 1 Scene 5 and Act 2 Scene 3?

22	*warrant*: believe.
23	*in my conscience*: quite honestly.
25	*I would*: I wish.

From lines 27–30 Feste makes comments about how Olivia would act in marriage. Consider also the statements Viola makes about Feste from lines 51–59.

What do Feste's comments suggest about Olivia's character?

29	*pilchards*: small herrings.
31	*late*: recently.
32	*the orb*: the earth.
33–4	*I would . . . mistress*: I should be sorry if there were not a fool (i.e. Viola) with your master as often as with my mistress.
35	*your wisdom*: your wise self.
36	*an' . . . thee*: if you make fun of me, I won't have anything more to do with you.
36–7	*Hold . . . thee*: here's something for you to spend.

3:1

OLIVIA's *garden*
Enter **VIOLA** *and* **FESTE,** *who plays on his pipe and tabor*

VIOLA	Save thee, friend, and thy music! Dost thou live by thy tabor?
FESTE	No, sir, I live by the church.
VIOLA	Art thou a churchman?
FESTE	No such matter, sir. I do live by the church, for I do live at my house, and my house doth stand by the church. 5
VIOLA	So thou mayst say the king lies by a beggar, if a beggar dwell near him; or the church stands by thy tabor, if thy tabor stand by the church.
FESTE	You have said, sir. To see this age! A sentence is but a chev'ril glove to a good wit—how quickly the wrong side may be 10 turned outward!
VIOLA	Nay, that's certain: they that dally nicely with words may quickly make them wanton.
FESTE	I would therefore my sister had had no name, sir.
VIOLA	Why, man? 15
FESTE	Why, sir, her name's a word, and to dally with that word might make my sister wanton. But indeed, words are very rascals, since bonds disgraced them.
VIOLA	Thy reason, man?
FESTE	Troth, sir, I can yield you none without words, and words 20 are grown so false, I am loath to prove reason with them.
VIOLA	I warrant thou art a merry fellow, and car'st for nothing.
FESTE	Not so, sir, I do care for something; but in my conscience, sir, I do not care for you: if that be to care for nothing, sir, I would it would make you invisible. 25
VIOLA	Art not thou the Lady Olivia's fool?
FESTE	No indeed sir, the Lady Olivia has no folly. She will keep no fool, sir, till she be married, and fools are as like husbands as pilchards are to herrings: the husband's the bigger. I am indeed not her fool, but her corrupter of words. 30
VIOLA	I saw thee late at the Count Orsino's.
FESTE	Foolery, sir, does walk about the orb like the sun: it shines everywhere. I would be sorry, sir, but the fool should be as oft with your master as with my mistress. I think I saw your wisdom there. 35
VIOLA	Nay, an' thou pass upon me, I'll no more with thee. Hold, there's expenses for thee.

38   *commodity*: consignment, delivery.

39   *troth*: truth.

41   *these*: i.e. coins.

42   *put to use*: invested.

43–4   *Lord ... Troilus*: Pandarus introduced his niece Cressida to Troilus during the Trojan War; the story is the subject of Shakespeare's play *Troilus and Cressida*, and of poems by Chaucer and Henryson.

46   *begging ... a beggar*: I was only asking for a beggar because that's what Cressida was; in Henryson's *The Testament of Cresseid* the heroine becomes a leper and is forced to beg for her living.

47   *conster*: construe, explain.

49   *welkin*: sky.
        element: sky.

50   *overworn*: over-used, stale.

52   *craves*: requires.

53   *their ... jests*: the mood of the people he is clowning for.

54   *quality*: social status.
        time: occasion.

55   *like ... feather*: like the wild hawk, swoop down on every prey (i.e. neglect no opportunity for jesting).

56   *practice*: skill.

57   *art*: profession.

58   *fit*: appropriate.

59   *folly-fall'n*: having fallen to folly.
        quite taint: completely spoil.

62   *Dieu ... monsieur*: God keep you, sir; Sir Andrew remembers a little French.

63   *Et ... serviteur*: and you too: at your service.

65   *encounter*: go to meet.

66   *trade*: business.

67   *bound to*: going towards.
        list: limit, destination.

69   *Taste*: try.

70   *understand me*: stand under me.

72   *to go*: to walk.

73   *answer*: obey.
        with ... entrance: by walking inside (with a pun on 'gate').
        prevented: forestalled.

Gives him a coin

FESTE	Now Jove, in his next commodity of hair, send thee a beard!
VIOLA	By my troth, I'll tell thee, I am almost sick for one—[*Aside*] though I would not have it grow on my chin. Is thy lady within? 40
FESTE	Would not a pair of these have bred, sir?
VIOLA	Yes, being kept together, and put to use.
FESTE	I would play Lord Pandarus of Phrygia, sir, to bring a Cressida to this Troilus.
VIOLA	I understand you, sir, 'tis well begged. 45

Gives him another coin

FESTE	The matter, I hope, is not great, sir, begging but a beggar: Cressida was a beggar. My lady is within, sir. I will conster to them whence you come; who you are and what you would are out of my welkin—I might say 'element', but the word is overworn. [*Exit* 50
VIOLA	This fellow is wise enough to play the fool, And to do that well, craves a kind of wit: He must observe their mood on whom he jests, The quality of persons, and the time, And, like the haggard, check at every feather 55 That comes before his eye. This is a practice As full of labour as a wise man's art: For folly that he wisely shows is fit; But wise men, folly-fall'n, quite taint their wit.

Enter **SIR TOBY** *and* **SIR ANDREW**

SIR TOBY	Save you, gentleman. 60
VIOLA	And you, sir.
SIR ANDREW	*Dieu vous garde, monsieur.*
VIOLA	*Et vous aussi: votre serviteur.*
SIR ANDREW	I hope, sir, you are, and I am yours.
SIR TOBY	Will you encounter the house? My niece is desirous you 65 should enter, if your trade be to her.
VIOLA	I am bound to your niece, sir; I mean, she is the list of my voyage.
SIR TOBY	Taste your legs, sir, put them to motion.
VIOLA	My legs do better understand me, sir, than I understand what 70 you mean by bidding me taste my legs.
SIR TOBY	I mean, to go, sir, to enter.
VIOLA	I will answer you with gait and entrance; but we are prevented.

77	*My matter*: what I have to say.
	hath no voice: cannot be spoken.
79	*pregnant*: receptive.
	vouchsafed: attentive.
79–80	*get . . . ready*: keep them all in mind; perhaps he writes in a notebook.
81	*hearing*: audience, meeting.
86	*'Twas . . . world*: the world has not been a happy place.
87	*lowly . . . compliment*: fake humility was called flattery.
89	*he . . . be yours*: he is your servant, and what he owns must necessarily be yours.
91	*For*: as for.
	on: about.
92	*Would they were blanks*: I would rather they were empty
93	*whet*: sharpen, excite.
98	*solicit*: argue about.
99	*music . . . spheres*: heavenly harmony (made by the rotation of the planets in their orbits).
101	*Give . . . you*: please let me speak.
102	*After . . . here*: after you had bewitched me last time you were here.
103	*abuse*: deceive, insult.
105	*hard construction*: severe judgement.
106	*that*: i.e. the ring.
107	*none of yours*: was not yours.
108–10	*Have . . . think*: Olivia pictures herself as a bear tied to the stake (see picture p. 82) and tormented by all the unrestrained thoughts that a cruel heart can devise.
110	*receiving*: understanding.
111	*a cypress*: a transparent veil.
114	*degree*: step; 'grize' in the next line has the same meaning.

Enter **OLIVIA** *and* **MARIA**

	Most excellent accomplished lady, the heavens rain odours	
	on you!	75
SIR ANDREW	That youth's a rare courtier: 'rain odours'—well!	
VIOLA	My matter hath no voice, lady, but to your own most pregnant	
	and vouchsafed ear.	
SIR ANDREW	'Odours', 'pregnant', and 'vouchsafed': I'll get 'em all three all	
	ready.	80
OLIVIA	Let the garden door be shut, and leave me to my hearing.	

                                      [*Exeunt* **SIR TOBY**, **SIR ANDREW**, *and* **MARIA**

	Give me your hand, sir.	
VIOLA	My duty, madam, and most humble service.	
OLIVIA	What is your name?	
VIOLA	Cesario is your servant's name, fair princess.	85
OLIVIA	My servant, sir? 'Twas never merry world	
	Since lowly feigning was call'd compliment:	
	Y'are servant to the Count Orsino, youth.	
VIOLA	And he is yours, and his must needs be yours:	
	Your servant's servant is your servant, madam.	90
OLIVIA	For him, I think not on him; for his thoughts,	
	Would they were blanks, rather than fill'd with me.	
VIOLA	Madam, I come to whet your gentle thoughts	
	On his behalf.	
OLIVIA	O, by your leave, I pray you!	95
	I bade you never speak again of him;	
	But would you undertake another suit,	
	I had rather hear you to solicit that,	
	Than music from the spheres.	
VIOLA	Dear lady—	100
OLIVIA	Give me leave, beseech you. I did send,	
	After the last enchantment you did here,	
	A ring in chase of you. So did I abuse	
	Myself, my servant, and, I fear me, you.	
	Under your hard construction must I sit,	105
	To force that on you in a shameful cunning	
	Which you knew none of yours. What might you think?	
	Have you not set mine honour at the stake,	
	And baited it with all th' unmuzzled thoughts	
	That tyrannous heart can think? To one of your receiving	110
	Enough is shown; a cypress, not a bosom,	
	Hides my heart. So, let me hear you speak.	
VIOLA	I pity you.	
OLIVIA	That's a degree to love.	

115	*vulgar proof*: common experience.
117	*'tis ... again*: I can smile again (because her enemy shows pity).
118	*how ... proud*: the deprived are so quick to think well of themselves (Olivia is ironic).
121	*upbraids*: reproaches.
123	*is ... harvest*: has ripened to maturity.
124	*like*: likely.
	proper: handsome.
126	*westward ho*: the cry of Thames boatmen for passengers going towards Westminster.
127	*Grace ... disposition*: the blessing of heaven and peace of mind.
128	*You'll nothing*: you have no message.
131	*you do ... are*: a) you forget that you are a noblewoman; b) you do not imagine you are in love with a woman.
132	*the ... you*: i.e. that you are not what you appear to be.
134	*I would ... be*: I wish you were what I want you to be (i.e Olivia's lover).
136	*I am your fool*: you're making a fool of me.
137–8	*what ... lip*: how beautiful he looks with his lips showing angry contempt.
139	*A ... guilt*: the guilt of a murderer.
140	*love ... hid*: love that tries to hide itself.
	Love ... noon: the most secret love is as clear as midday.
142	*maidhood*: virginity.
143	*maugre ... pride*: despite all your unkindness.
144	*Nor ... reason*: neither intelligence nor sense.
145–6	*Do not ... cause*: don't force yourself to deduce from this argument ('clause') that because ('For that') I am courting you, there is no need for you to court me.
147	*reason ... fetter*: join one reason to another like this.
151	*nor never none*: and there will never be any woman.
154	*deplore*: weep out.
155	*move*: persuade.

Is Olivia's behaviour towards Cesario typical of women of that era? Justify your answer.

Class activity:

Discuss the irony in Olivia's profession of love for Cesario.

VIOLA	No, not a grize: for 'tis a vulgar proof	115
	That very oft we pity enemies.	
OLIVIA	Why then methinks 'tis time to smile again.	
	O world, how apt the poor are to be proud!	
	If one should be a prey, how much the better	
	To fall before the lion than the wolf! [*Clock strikes*]	120
	The clock upbraids me with the waste of time.	
	Be not afraid, good youth, I will not have you.	
	And yet when wit and youth is come to harvest	
	Your wife is like to reap a proper man.	
	There lies your way, due west.	125
VIOLA	Then westward ho!	
	Grace and good disposition attend your ladyship.	
	You'll nothing, madam, to my lord by me?	
OLIVIA	Stay!	
	I prithee, tell me what thou think'st of me.	130
VIOLA	That you do think you are not what you are.	
OLIVIA	If I think so, I think the same of you.	
VIOLA	Then think you right; I am not what I am.	
OLIVIA	I would you were as I would have you be.	
VIOLA	Would it be better, madam, than I am?	135
	I wish it might, for now I am your fool.	
OLIVIA	[*Aside*] O what a deal of scorn looks beautiful	
	In the contempt and anger of his lip!	
	A murd'rous guilt shows not itself more soon	
	Than love that would seem hid. Love's night is noon.	140
	Cesario, by the roses of the spring,	
	By maidhood, honour, truth, and everything,	
	I love thee so that, maugre all thy pride,	
	Nor wit nor reason can my passion hide.	
	Do not extort thy reasons from this clause.	145
	For that I woo, thou therefore hast no cause;	
	But rather reason thus with reason fetter:	
	Love sought is good, but given unsought is better.	
VIOLA	By innocence I swear, and by my youth,	
	I have one heart, one bosom, and one truth,	150
	And that no woman has; nor never none	
	Shall mistress be of it, save I alone.	
	And so adieu, good madam; never more	
	Will I my master's tears to you deplore.	
OLIVIA	Yet come again: for thou perhaps mayst move	155
	That heart which now abhors, to like his love.	
	[*Exeunt*	

3:2

Sir Andrew suspects that Olivia is not interested in him, as she is more interested in the Duke's servant. He threatens to go home. Sir Toby encourages him to stay and challenge Cesario to a duel.

1	*jot*: moment.
2	*dear venom*: sweet poison.
3	*yield*: give.
4	*Marry*: indeed.
6	*the while*: at the time.
8	*argument*: proof.
9	*'Slight*: by God's light.
10	*legitimate*: logically admissible. *oaths*: sworn testimony; Fabian and Sir Toby try to confuse Sir Andrew.
12	*grand-jurymen*: The grand-jury decided whether a case deserved a proper trial.
12–13	*before . . . sailor*: before the Flood.
15	*dormouse*: a very small mouse which sleeps all winter.
17	*accosted*: approached (see Act 1, Scene 3, line 40 note).
17–18	*fire-new . . . mint*: as brilliant as newly-minted coins.
18	*banged*: beaten.
19	*looked . . . hand*: expected from you. *balked*: refused.
20	*double gilt*: gilt-plate twice washed with gold.
22	*hang . . . beard*: Fabian alludes to the Dutchman William Barents, who made a famous arctic voyage in 1596–7.
23	*laudable attempt*: special effort. *valour or policy*: bravery or cunning.
24	*An't*: if it. *policy I hate*: I hate intrigue.
24–5	*I had as lief*: I would as willingly.
25	*Brownist*: a Puritan sect (founded by Robert Browne in the 16th century).
26	*build me*: go and build; 'me' is used merely for emphasis
27	*to fight*: by offering to fight.
28	*take note*: notice.
29	*love-broker*: marriage-broker.

Toby Belch is aware that Sir Andrew is a coward, yet he encourages him to challenge Cesario to a fight.

Why would Toby encourage Andrew to fight Cesario knowing that Andrew is afraid? What does this tell you about Sir Toby?

33	*curst*: fierce.
34	*invention*: untruth.
35–6	*If thou . . . amiss*: it wouldn't be a bad idea to address him about three times as 'thou' (a form used only to intimate and inferiors).
36	*lies*: falsehoods.

3:2

OLIVIA's *house*
Enter SIR TOBY, SIR ANDREW, *and* FABIAN

SIR ANDREW	No, faith, I'll not stay a jot longer.
SIR TOBY	Thy reason, dear venom, give thy reason.
FABIAN	You must needs yield your reason, Sir Andrew.
SIR ANDREW	Marry, I saw your niece do more favours to the Count's serving-man than ever she bestowed upon me. I saw't i' th' orchard. 5
SIR TOBY	Did she see thee the while, old boy, tell me that?
SIR ANDREW	As plain as I see you now.
FABIAN	This was a great argument of love in her toward you.
SIR ANDREW	'Slight! Will you make an ass o' me?
FABIAN	I will prove it legitimate, sir, upon the oaths of judgment and 10 reason.
SIR TOBY	And they have been grand-jurymen since before Noah was a sailor.
FABIAN	She did show favour to the youth in your sight only to exasperate you, to awake your dormouse valour, to put fire in 15 your heart, and brimstone in your liver. You should then have accosted her, and with some excellent jests, fire-new from the mint, you should have banged the youth into dumbness. This was looked for at your hand, and this was balked. The double gilt of this opportunity you let time wash off, and you 20 are now sailed into the north of my lady's opinion, where you will hang like an icicle on a Dutchman's beard, unless you do redeem it by some laudable attempt, either of valour or policy.
SIR ANDREW	An't be any way, it must be with valour, for policy I hate: I had as lief be a Brownist as a politician. 25
SIR TOBY	Why then, build me thy fortunes upon the basis of valour. Challenge me the Count's youth to fight with him; hurt him in eleven places: my niece shall take note of it; and assure thyself there is no love-broker in the world can more prevail in man's commendation with woman than report of valour. 30
FABIAN	There is no way but this, Sir Andrew.
SIR ANDREW	Will either of you bear me a challenge to him?
SIR TOBY	Go, write it in a martial hand. Be curst and brief: it is no matter how witty, so it be eloquent and full of invention. Taunt him with the licence of ink. If thou thou'st him some thrice, it shall 35 not be amiss; and as many lies as will lie in thy sheet of paper,

37   *bed of Ware*: a famous carved bed about 3 metres square in Ware, Hertfordshire (now in the Victoria and Albert Museum, London).

38   *set 'em down*: write them down.
    about it: get on with it.
    gall: a) venom; b) a growth on oak-trees used in making ink.

39   *goose-pen*: pen made from the quill of a goose (proverbially a foolish bird).

42   *cubiculo*: bed-chamber.

43   *dear manikin*: precious plaything; Sir Toby plays on 'dear' = expensive.

44   *some ... strong*: a good two thousand (ducats).

45   *rare*: extraordinary.

46   *by ... stir on*: do everything I can to provoke.

47   *wainropes*: cart-ropes.
    hale: drag.

48   *opened*: dissected.

49   *blood ... liver*: A bloodless liver was thought to be a sign of cowardice.

50   *anatomy*: corpse.

51   *opposite*: opponent.
    visage: face.

52   *presage*: promise.

53   *wren*: a tiny brown bird; the last chick to hatch is always the smallest.

54   *spleen*: a fit of laughter (thought to arise from the spleen).

55   *Yond gull*: that idiot.

56   *renegado*: heretic.

56–7 *means ... rightly*: hopes for salvation through orthodox Christian faith.

57–8 *impossible ... grossness*: grossly incredible statements.

The audience and the other characters are aware of the trick being played on Malvolio, but he is not aware. Comment on the technique Shakespeare uses.

Show how Shakespeare continues the theme of disguise.

60   *like ... church*: like an old-fashioned schoolmaster who teaches his class in the church.

61   *dogged him*: followed him closely.

63–4 *more lines ... Indies*: a new map, published 1599, showed more details of the Indies than earlier maps, and included a network of 'rhumb' lines of navigation.

	although the sheet were big enough for the bed of Ware in England, set 'em down. Go, about it. Let there be gall enough in thy ink, though thou write with a goose-pen, no matter. About it!	40
SIR ANDREW	Where shall I find you?	
SIR TOBY	We'll call thee at thy cubiculo. Go! [*Exit* **SIR ANDREW**	
FABIAN	This is a dear manikin to you, Sir Toby.	
SIR TOBY	I have been dear to him, lad, some two thousand strong, or so.	
FABIAN	We shall have a rare letter from him—but you'll not deliver't—	45
SIR TOBY	Never trust me then? and by all means stir on the youth to an answer. I think oxen and wainropes cannot hale them together. For Andrew, if he were opened and you find so much blood in his liver as will clog the foot of a flea, I'll eat the rest of th' anatomy.	50
FABIAN	And his opposite, the youth, bears in his visage no great presage of cruelty.	

Enter **MARIA**

SIR TOBY	Look where the youngest wren of nine comes.	
MARIA	If you desire the spleen, and will laugh yourselves into stitches, follow me. Yond gull Malvolio is turned heathen, a very renegado; for there is no Christian, that means to be saved by believing rightly, can ever believe such impossible passages of grossness. He's in yellow stockings!	55
SIR TOBY	And cross-gartered?	
MARIA	Most villainous: like a pedant that keeps a school i' th' church. I have dogged him like his murderer. He does obey every point of the letter that I dropped to betray him. He does smile his face into more lines than is in the new map with the augmentation of the Indies: you have not seen such a thing as 'tis! I can hardly forbear hurling things at him—I know my lady will strike him. If she do, he'll smile, and take't for a great favour.	60 65
SIR TOBY	Come bring us, bring us where he is. [*Exeunt*	

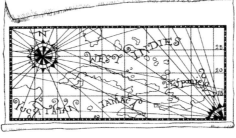

3:3

Sebastian decides to go sightseeing and invites Antonio to come along. Antonio refuses, but insists on lending him money.

1	*by my will*: willingly.
2	*you make . . . pains*: you enjoy taking this trouble.
3	*chide*: scold.
4	*stay behind you*: let you go without me.
5	*filed steel*: filèd; the sharp point of a steel spur.
6	*not all*: it was not only.
6–7	*so much . . . voyage*: enough love to make me undertake a longer journey.
8	*jealousy*: anxiety.
9	*skilless in*: a stranger in.
9–11	*to a stranger . . . unhospitable*: Antonio's view of Illyria is in marked contrast to the impression created by the two noble households.
12	*The rather*: even more readily.
13	*in your pursuit*: to follow you.
16	*good turns*: kindnesses.
17	*shuffled off*: passed over. *uncurrent pay*: valueless repayment.
18	*were . . . firm*: if my wealth were as great as my sense of being indebted.
19	*dealing*: treatment. *What's to do*: what shall we do.
20	*relics*: sights, antiquities.
22	*'tis long to night*: there's a long time before nightfall.
25	*renown*: make famous.
26	*Would . . . me*: you'll have to excuse me.
28	*the Count his*: the Count's.
29	*service*: fighting. *of such note*: so considerable.
30	*ta'en*: arrested. *scarce be answer'd*: be hard to account for.
31	*Belike*: I suppose.

Antonio explains to Sebastian why he cannot go with him on his sightseeing tour (lines 27–39).

What is the dramatic significance of his explanation?

What dramatic technique does Shakespeare use in this situation?

33–4	*Albeit . . . argument*: although the nature of the occasion and the dispute might well have given us cause for bloodshed.
35–6	*It might . . . them*: perhaps the quarrel has since been settled by repaying what we took from them.
36	*traffic's sake*: the sake of trading.
37	*stood out*: refused to pay.
38	*lapsed*: lapsèd; apprehended.
40	*open*: conspicuously.

3:3

The street
Enter **Sebastian** *and* **Antonio**

Sebastian I would not by my will have troubled you,
But since you make your pleasure of your pains,
I will no further chide you.

Antonio I could not stay behind you. My desire,
More sharp than filed steel, did spur me forth: 5
And not all love to see you (though so much
As might have drawn one to a longer voyage)
But jealousy what might befall your travel,
Being skilless in these parts: which to a stranger,
Unguided and unfriended, often prove 10
Rough and unhospitable. My willing love
The rather by these arguments of fear
Set forth in your pursuit.

Sebastian   My kind Antonio,
I can no other answer make, but thanks, 15
And thanks, and ever thanks; and oft good turns
Are shuffled off with such uncurrent pay:
But were my worth, as is my conscience, firm,
You should find better dealing. What's to do?
Shall we go see the relics of this town? 20

Antonio Tomorrow, sir; best first go see your lodging.

Sebastian I am not weary, and 'tis long to night.
I pray you, let us satisfy our eyes
With the memorials and the things of fame
That do renown this city. 25

Antonio   Would you'd pardon me:
I do not without danger walk these streets.
Once in a sea-fight 'gainst the Count his galleys,
I did some service—of such note indeed,
That were I ta'en here it would scarce be answer'd. 30

Sebastian Belike you slew great number of his people.

Antonio Th' offence is not of such a bloody nature,
Albeit the quality of the time and quarrel
Might well have given us bloody argument.
It might have since been answer'd in repaying 35
What we took from them, which for traffic's sake
Most of our city did. Only myself stood out,
For which, if I be lapsed in this place,
I shall pay dear.

Sebastian   Do not then walk too open. 40

41   *It ... me*: I don't intend to.

42   *Elephant*: the name of an inn (spelled 'Oliphant') near Shakespeare's Bankside theatre.

43   *bespeak our diet*: order our meals.

44   *beguile the time*: amuse yourself.

45   *have me*: find me.

46   *Why I your purse?*: Why should I take your money.

47   *Haply*: perhaps.
        some toy: some little thing.

48–9   *your store ... markets*: I don't think your own money ('store') is enough for casual purchases.

50   *purse-bearer*: treasurer.

Class activity:

Based on Antonio's behaviour towards Sebastian, write down at least three characteristics that Antonio displays. Give reasons for your answer.

3:4

Malvolio appears, dressed strangely and acting strangely. Olivia is puzzled and asks Sir Toby to take control of him. Toby and Fabian go to great lengths to ensure that the two duelists are afraid of each other. Antonio sees Cesario, mistakes him for Sebastian, and comes to his rescue. Antonio is captured and asks "Sebastian" for his money. "Sebastian" does not know what he is talking about.

1   *he says*: if he says (Olivia visualises a possible situation).

2   *of*: on.

3   *youth*: young men; Olivia cynically adapts the proverb 'better to buy than to borrow'.

5   *sad and civil*: sober and serious.

9   *possessed*: taken over by the devil, mad.

12   *were best*: would be advised.

18   *upon a sad occasion*: about a serious matter.

21   *sonnet*: song: Malvolio quotes the first line of a popular ballad.

ANTONIO	It doth not fit me. Hold, sir, here's my purse.
	In the south suburbs, at the Elephant,
	Is best to lodge. I will bespeak our diet
	Whiles you beguile the time, and feed your knowledge
	With viewing of the town. There shall you have me. **45**
SEBASTIAN	Why I your purse?
ANTONIO	Haply your eye shall light upon some toy
	You have desire to purchase: and your store,
	I think, is not for idle markets, sir.
SEBASTIAN	I'll be your purse-bearer, and leave you for **50**
	An hour.
ANTONIO	To th' Elephant.
SEBASTIAN	I do remember.

[Exeunt separately

3:4

OLIVIA's *garden*
Enter **OLIVIA** *and* **MARIA**

OLIVIA	*[Aside]* I have sent after him, he says he'll come:
	How shall I feast him? What bestow of him?
	For youth is bought more oft than begg'd or borrow'd.
	I speak too loud.—
	Where's Malvolio? He is sad and civil, **5**
	And suits well for a servant with my fortunes:
	Where is Malvolio?
MARIA	He's coming, madam, but in very strange manner. He is sure possessed, madam.
OLIVIA	Why, what's the matter? Does he rave? **10**
MARIA	No, madam, he does nothing but smile: your ladyship were best to have some guard about you if he come, for sure the man is tainted in's wits.
OLIVIA	Go call him hither. *[Exit* Maria] I am as mad as he
	If sad and merry madness equal be. **15**

Enter **MALVOLIO** *with* **MARIA**

	How now, Malvolio?
MALVOLIO	Sweet Lady, ho, ho!
OLIVIA	Smil'st thou? I sent for thee upon a sad occasion.
MALVOLIO	Sad, lady? I could be sad: this does make some obstruction in the blood, this cross-gartering; but what of that? If it please **20** the eye of one, it is with me as the very true sonnet is: *'Please one, and please all'*.

23   *how dost thou*: how are you.

24   *Not ... mind*: not melancholy.
       though ... legs: although my legs are yellow (a colour associated with melancholy).

24–5   *It did ... hands*: the letter reached the right man's hands.

26   *the sweet Roman hand*: the elegant italic script (more fashionable at this time than the ordinary English handwriting).

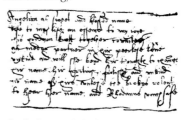

Elizabethan English script

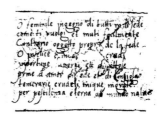

Italian style of handwriting

28   *Ay, sweetheart ... thee*: a line from a popular song.

32   *At your request*: must I answer someone like you; Malvolio is obeying the injunction to be 'surly with servants' (Act 2, Scene 5, line 125).
       daws: jackdaws.

‖ *What is Malvolio's perception of himself?*

Class activity:

Re-enact this scene with the use of costumes. Note the reaction of your classmates.

---

46   *thou art made*: your fortune is made—but Olivia thinks Malvolio is saying that she is 'mad'.

49   *very ... madness*: a real fit of lunacy; the phrase was proverbial.

‖ *Give an example of dramatic irony in this scene with Malvolio and Olivia.*

OLIVIA	Why, how dost thou, man? What is the matter with thee?
MALVOLIO	Not black in my mind, though yellow in my legs. It did come to his hands, and commands shall be executed. I think we do know the sweet Roman hand.
OLIVIA	Wilt thou go to bed, Malvolio?
MALVOLIO	To bed? *Ay, sweetheart, and I'll come to thee.*
OLIVIA	God comfort thee! Why dost thou smile so, and kiss thy hand so oft?
MARIA	How do you, Malvolio?
MALVOLIO	At your request? Yes, nightingales answer daws!
MARIA	Why appear you with this ridiculous boldness before my lady?
MALVOLIO	'Be not afraid of greatness': 'twas well writ.
OLIVIA	What mean'st thou by that, Malvolio?
MALVOLIO	'Some are born great—'
OLIVIA	Ha?
MALVOLIO	'Some achieve greatness—'
OLIVIA	What say'st thou?
MALVOLIO	'And some have greatness thrust upon them.'
OLIVIA	Heaven restore thee!
MALVOLIO	'Remember who commended thy yellow stockings—'
OLIVIA	Thy yellow stockings?
MALVOLIO	'And wished to see thee cross-gartered.'
OLIVIA	Cross-gartered?
MALVOLIO	'Go to, thou art made, if thou desir'st to be so—'
OLIVIA	Am I made?
MALVOLIO	'If not, let me see thee a servant still.'
OLIVIA	Why, this is very midsummer madness.

25

30

35

40

45

The peak of the plot: Malvolio in yellow stockings.

111

51   *I ... back*: I could hardly restrain him.

55   *miscarry*: come to harm.

57   *come near*: begin to understand.

58   *to look to*: to take care of.
      concurs: agrees.

59   *stubborn*: rude.

63   *consequently*: accordingly.
      sets down: describes.

64   *sad*: serious.
      reverend carriage: dignified deportment.

65   *in ... note*: in the style of some important personage.

66   *limed her*: caught her (like a bird on a branch sticky with lime).

67   *Fellow*: Malvolio persuades himself that Olivia is referring to him as her equal.

68   *degree*: rank (as steward).

69   *adheres*: accords.

69–70   *no dram ... scruple*: not the tiniest little amount; 'dram' and 'scruple' are apothecary's weights.

69   *dram*: 1/3 ounce (1 ounce = 28 grams).
      scruple: a) 1/3 dram; b) doubt.

70   *incredulous*: incredible.

72   *full ... hopes*: fulfilment of all my hopes.

74   *sanctity*: Sir Toby invokes divine protection before tackling the supposed devil possessing Malvolio.

75   *drawn in little*: a) portrayed in miniature; b) contracted into one body.
      Legion: the name claimed by the devil possessing a madman in St Mark's Gospel (5:8–9).

79   *discard*: reject.
      private: privacy.

80   *hollow*: a) deceptively; b) spookily.

83–4   *Let me alone*: leave me to handle him alone.

85   *defy*: renounce.

89   *Carry his water*: take a urine specimen.
      wise woman: i.e. a 'good' witch, skilled in occult arts and sciences.

What is ironic about the situation where Olivia gives Malvolio over to Sir Toby and the others for pastoral care in his assumed madness?

Enter **SERVANT**

SERVANT	Madam, the young gentleman of the Count Orsino's is returned; I could hardly entreat him back. He attends your ladyship's pleasure.	50
OLIVIA	I'll come to him. [*Exit* **SERVANT**] Good Maria, let this fellow be looked to. Where's my cousin Toby? Let some of my people have a special care of him; I would not have him miscarry for the half of my dowry.	55

[*Exeunt* **OLIVIA** *and* **MARIA** *different ways*

MALVOLIO	O ho, do you come near me now? No worse man than Sir Toby to look to me! This concurs directly with the letter: she sends him on purpose, that I may appear stubborn to him; for she incites me to that in the letter. 'Cast thy humble slough,' says she; 'be opposite with a kinsman, surly with servants, let thy tongue tang arguments of state, put thyself into the trick of singularity'—and consequently sets down the manner how: as, a sad face, a reverend carriage, a slow tongue, in the habit of some sir of note, and so forth. I have limed her, but it is Jove's doing, and Jove make me thankful! And when she went away now, 'Let this fellow be looked to'. 'Fellow'! Not Malvolio, nor after my degree, but 'fellow'. Why, everything adheres together, that no dram of a scruple, no scruple of a scruple, no obstacle, no incredulous or unsafe circumstance—what can be said?—nothing that can be can come between me and the full prospect of my hopes. Well, Jove, not I, is the doer of this, and he is to be thanked.	60 65 70

Enter **SIR TOBY, FABIAN**, *and* **MARIA**

SIR TOBY	Which way is he, in the name of sanctity? If all the devils of hell be drawn in little, and Legion himself possessed him, yet I'll speak to him.	75
FABIAN	Here he is, here he is. How is't with you, sir? How is't with you, man?	
MALVOLIO	Go off, I discard you. Let me enjoy my private. Go off.	
MARIA	Lo, how hollow the fiend speaks within him! Did not I tell you? Sir Toby, my lady prays you to have a care of him.	80
MALVOLIO	[*Aside*] Ah ha! Does she so?	
SIR TOBY	Go to, go to: peace, peace, we must deal gently with him. Let me alone. How do you, Malvolio? How is't with you? What, man, defy the devil! Consider, he's an enemy to mankind.	85
MALVOLIO	Do you know what you say?	
MARIA	La you, an' you speak ill of the devil, how he takes it at heart! Pray God he be not bewitched!	
FABIAN	Carry his water to th' wise woman.	

90	*if I live*: as sure as I'm alive.
95	*move*: excite.
96	*rough*: violent.
98–100	*bawcock ... chuck ... biddy*: fine fellow ... chicken ... chickabiddy (terms of endearment spoken to children).
100–1	*'tis not ... Satan*: it's not right for a sensible man ('gravity') to be playing children's games with the devil.
101	*cherry-pit*: a game of throwing cherry-stones into a hole. *foul collier*: dirty coalman (traditionally said to be black in heart as well as in appearance).
103	*minx*: shameless woman.
105–6	*I am ... element*: I am out of your sphere, I am superior to you.
106	*hereafter*: later.
108–9	*If this ... fiction*: Shakespeare draws attention to the unreality of theatrical illusion.
108	*played*: performed. *could*: would.
109	*an improbable fiction*: something that could never happen.
110	*genius*: nature, guiding spirit. *taken*: caught. *device*: plot.
111	*take air*: becomes known, comes into the open. *taint*: gets spoiled.
114	*we'll ... bound*: This was standard treatment of the insane.
115	*carry it thus*: keep this up.
116	*pastime*: amusement.
118	*bring ... bar*: let our trick be brought to the bar for public judgement.
119	*finder*: judge, one who can identify.
120	*matter ... morning*: games for a holiday (especially the morris games of May Day).
121–2	*vinegar and pepper in't*: it is highly spiced (= insolent).
123	*saucy*: cheeky—with a play on 'vinegar and pepper'.
124	*I warrant him*: I can assure you.
125	*whatsoever*: of whatever degree. *thou*: Sir Andrew uses the familiar form—in accordance with Sir Toby's advice (Act 3, Scene 2, lines 35–36).

MARIA	Marry, and it shall be done tomorrow morning, if I live. My lady would not lose him for more than I'll say.	90
MALVOLIO	How now, mistress?	
MARIA	O Lord!	
SIR TOBY	Prithee hold thy peace, this is not the way. Do you not see you move him? Let me alone with him.	95
FABIAN	No way but gentleness, gently, gently: the fiend is rough, and will not be roughly used.	
SIR TOBY	Why, how now, my bawcock? How dost thou, chuck?	
MALVOLIO	Sir!	
SIR TOBY	Ay, biddy, come with me. What, man, 'tis not for gravity to play at cherry-pit with Satan. Hang him, foul collier!	100
MARIA	Get him to say his prayers, good Sir Toby, get him to pray.	
MALVOLIO	My prayers, minx!	
MARIA	No, I warrant you, he will not hear of godliness.	
MALVOLIO	Go hang yourselves all. You are idle, shallow things; I am not of your element. You shall know more hereafter.	105

[Exit

SIR TOBY	Is't possible?	
FABIAN	If this were played upon a stage now, I could condemn it as an improbable fiction.	
SIR TOBY	His very genius hath taken the infection of the device, man.	110
MARIA	Nay, pursue him now, lest the device take air, and taint.	
FABIAN	Why, we shall make him mad indeed.	
MARIA	The house will be the quieter.	
SIR TOBY	Come, we'll have him in a dark room and bound. My niece is already in the belief that he's mad: we may carry it thus for our pleasure, and his penance, till our very pastime, tired out of breath, prompt us to have mercy on him; at which time we will bring the device to the bar, and crown thee for a finder of madmen. But see, but see!	115

Enter **SIR ANDREW**

FABIAN	More matter for a May morning!	120
SIR ANDREW	Here's the challenge, read it: I warrant there's vinegar and pepper in't.	
FABIAN	Is't so saucy?	
SIR ANDREW	Ay, is't, I warrant him: do but read.	
SIR TOBY	Give me. *[Reads] Youth, whatsoever thou art, thou art but a scurvy fellow.*	125
FABIAN	Good and valiant.	

128	*admire not*: do not marvel.
130	*keeps ... law*: protects you from legal action; Sir Andrew's gibes are surprisingly careful in their phrasing.
131	*uses*: treats.
132	*thou ... throat*: you are a complete liar (see Act 3, Scene 2 line 36).
134	*sense ... less*: The 'less' is not intended for Sir Andrew's hearing.
135	*chance*: good luck.
138	*like ... villain*: The terms could refer equally to 'thou' or to 'me': Sir Andrew maintains his ambiguity.
139	*o'th' windy side*: on the safe side; a seaman sails *with* the wind to avoid being driven on to the rocks.
141	*my ... better*: I have more hope of beating you. *look to*: take care of.
142	*as ... him*: if you treat him as a friend.
144	*move*: a) anger; b) propel.
146	*commerce*: conversation.
147	*scout me*: keep a look-out.
148	*bum-baily*: bailiff (who comes up behind the man he is arresting). *So*: as.
149	*draw*: draw your sword.
149–50	*comes to pass oft*: often happens.
150–1	*sharply twanged off*: pronounced boldly.
151	*gives ... approbation*: gives a man greater credit for courage.
152	*proof*: being put to the test.
153	*let me alone*: you can't beat me.
155	*gives him out*: shows him.
155–6	*of good ... breeding*: very intelligent and well-educated.
156	*his employment*: the way he is employed (as a messenger).
158	*breed*: give rise to.
159	*clodpole*: blockhead.
160–1	*set ... valour*: tell him that Aguecheek has a remarkable reputation for courage.
162	*aptly receive it*: be quick to understand it. *hideous*: fearful.
164	*cockatrices*: fabulous serpents which could kill their opponents with a single glance.
165	*give them way*: keep out of their way.
166	*and ... him*: then immediately go after him.

SIR TOBY	*Wonder not, nor admire not in thy mind, why I do call thee so, for I will show thee no reason for't.*
FABIAN	A good note; that keeps you from the blow of the law. 130
SIR TOBY	*Thou com'st to the Lady Olivia, and in my sight she uses thee kindly: but thou liest in thy throat; that is not the matter I challenge thee for.*
FABIAN	Very brief, and to exceeding good sense [*Aside*]-less!
SIR TOBY	*I will waylay thee going home, where if it be thy chance to kill* 135 *me—*
FABIAN	Good!
SIR TOBY	*Thou kill'st me like a rogue and a villain.*
FABIAN	Still you keep o' th' windy side of the law: good.
SIR TOBY	*Fare thee well, and God have mercy upon one of our souls! He* 140 *may have mercy upon mine, but my hope is better, and so look to thyself. Thy friend, as thou usest him, and thy sworn enemy,*
	Andrew Aguecheek.
	If this letter move him not, his legs cannot. I'll give't him.
MARIA	You may have very fit occasion for't. He is now in some 145 commerce with my lady, and will by and by depart.
SIR TOBY	So, Sir Andrew: scout me for him at the corner of the orchard, like a bum-baily. So soon as ever thou see'st him, draw, and as thou draw'st, swear horrible—for it comes to pass oft that a terrible oath, with a swaggering accent sharply 150 twanged off, gives manhood more approbation than ever proof itself would have earned him. Away!
SIR ANDREW	Nay, let me alone for swearing. [*Exit*
SIR TOBY	Now will not I deliver his letter. For the behaviour of the young gentleman gives him out to be of good capacity and 155 breeding: his employment between his lord and my niece confirms no less. Therefore this letter, being so excellently ignorant, will breed no terror in the youth: he will find it comes from a clodpole. But sir, I will deliver his challenge by word of mouth, set upon Aguecheek a notable report of 160 valour, and drive the gentleman (as I know his youth will aptly receive it) into a most hideous opinion of his rage, skill, fury, and impetuosity. This will so fright them both that they will kill one another by the look, like cockatrices.

Enter OLIVIA *and* VIOLA

FABIAN	Here he comes with your niece. Give them way till he take 165 leave, and presently after him.
SIR TOBY	I will meditate the while upon some horrid message for a challenge. [*Exeunt* SIR TOBY, FABIAN, *and* MARIA

170   *laid . . . out*: risked my reputation unwisely.

174   *'haviour*: behaviour.

176   *my picture*: Olivia's gift of a jewelled miniature recalls the unveiling of her 'picture' in *Act 1*, Scene 5.

179–80   *What . . . give*: you can't ask me for anything that, saving my honour, I wouldn't give you immediately.

184   *acquit you*: release you (from that gift).

186   *like thee*: in your likeness.

Shakespeare heightens suspense by increasing the tension in various ways (lines 187 onward).

Identify and explain two ways in which Shakespeare heightens the suspense.

How could this help the playwright?

189   *That . . . to't*: make use of whatever skill in fencing you have

190   *thou*: that you.

191   *intercepter*: adversary.
      despite: ill will.
      bloody . . . hunter: bloodthirsty like a dog hunting its prey
      attends: is lying in wait.

192   *Dismount thy tuck*: unsheathe your rapier.
      yare: prompt.

194   *to*: with.

195   *remembrance*: recollection.
      image: memory.

197–8   *if . . . price*: if you value your life at all.

199   *opposite*: opponent.

200   *furnish man withal*: equip a man with.

201   *what is he*: what rank is he.

202   *knight . . . rapier*: dubbed a knight with sword never drawn from its sheathe.

202–3   *carpet consideration*: for domestic (not military) service– and perhaps for payment.

203–4   *Souls . . . three*: he has killed three men.

204   *incensement*: rage.

206   *sepulchre*: burial.
      Hob, nob: have it or have it not.

207   *give't or take't*: kill or be killed.

OLIVIA	I have said too much unto a heart of stone,	
	And laid mine honour too unchary out.	170
	There's something in me that reproves my fault,	
	But such a headstrong potent fault it is	
	That it but mocks reproof.	
VIOLA	With the same 'haviour that your passion bears	
	Goes on my master's griefs.	175
OLIVIA	Here, wear this jewel for me, 'tis my picture:	
	Refuse it not, it hath no tongue to vex you.	
	And I beseech you come again tomorrow.	
	What shall you ask of me that I'll deny,	
	That honour sav'd may upon asking give?	180
VIOLA	Nothing but this: your true love for my master.	
OLIVIA	How with mine honour may I give him that	
	Which I have given to you?	
VIOLA	I will acquit you.	
OLIVIA	Well, come again tomorrow. Fare thee well;	185
	A fiend like thee might bear my soul to hell.	*[Exit*

Enter **SIR TOBY** *and* **FABIAN**

SIR TOBY	Gentleman, God save thee.	
VIOLA	And you, sir.	
SIR TOBY	That defence thou hast, betake thee to't. Of what nature	
	the wrongs are thou hast done him, I know not; but thy	190
	intercepter, full of despite, bloody as the hunter, attends	
	thee at the orchard-end. Dismount thy tuck, be yare in thy	
	preparation, for thy assailant is quick, skilful, and deadly.	
VIOLA	You mistake, sir; I am sure no man hath any quarrel to me:	
	my remembrance is very free and clear from any image of	195
	offence done to any man.	
SIR TOBY	You'll find it otherwise, I assure you. Therefore, if you hold	
	your life at any price, betake you to your guard; for your	
	opposite hath in him what youth, strength, skill, and wrath,	
	can furnish man withal.	200
VIOLA	I pray you, sir, what is he?	
SIR TOBY	He is knight dubbed with unhatched rapier, and on carpet	
	consideration, but he is a devil in private brawl. Souls and	
	bodies hath he divorced three, and his incensement at this	
	moment is so implacable that satisfaction can be none but	205
	by pangs of death and sepulchre. Hob, nob, is his word:	
	give't or take't.	

208–9	*desire . . . lady*: ask the lady to give me an escort.
210	*taste*: test.
211	*quirk*: peculiarity.
212	*derives itself*: is caused by.
	very competent: quite adequate.
213	*get you on*: go forward.
	his desire: a fight.
213–4	*Back you shall not*: you shall not go back.
214	*that*: the same duel.
215	*answer*: undertake.
216	*strip . . . naked*: unsheathe your sword.
	meddle: get involved.
217	*forswear . . . you*: stop wearing a sword (the sign of a gentleman).
218	*uncivil*: incorrect, mistaken.
218–9	*do . . . know of*: be so kind as to find out from.
220	*something . . . purpose*: the result of some negligence, nothing intentional.
224–5	*a mortal arbitrement*: a fight to the death to prove his case
	circumstance: details.

In lines 227–231 Fabian reports to Cesario that Sir Andrew is 'the most skillful, bloody, and fatal' opponent that he could encounter.

Pretend that you are Cesario. What emotions might you experience as a result of this report?

227	*to read . . . form*: to judge by outward appearance.
228	*like*: likely.
	in the . . . valour: when you put his courage to the test.
229	*bloody*: bloodthirsty. *fatal*: deadly.
	opposite: opponent.
232	*much bound*: greatly indebted.
233	*Sir Priest*: The usual designation of a university graduate ('Sir') was extended even to non-graduate clergymen.
234	*mettle*: courage.
235	*firago*: Sir Toby's mistaking of 'virago' = a warlike woman.
236	*pass*: fencing bout. *scabbard*: sheath.
237	*stuck in*: thrust through.
	mortal motion: deadly action.
238	*inevitable*: unavoidable.
	on the answer . . . you: on the return blow he stabs right home.
240	*Sophy*: Shah of Persia (see Act 2, Scene 5, line 154 note).
241	*Pox on't*: curse it.
244	*Plague on't*: damn it. *an*: if.
244–5	*cunning in fence*: skilful in fencing.
246	*let . . . slip*: overlook the matter.
247	*grey Capilet*: Elizabethans often included the colour of a horse when mentioning its name.

VIOLA	I will return again into the house, and desire some conduct of the lady. I am no fighter. I have heard of some kind of men that put quarrels purposely on others to taste their valour: belike this is a man of that quirk. 210
SIR TOBY	Sir, no. His indignation derives itself out of a very competent injury; therefore get you on, and give him his desire. Back you shall not to the house, unless you undertake that with me which with as much safety you might answer him. 215 Therefore on, or strip your sword stark naked: for meddle you must, that's certain, or forswear to wear iron about you.
VIOLA	This is as uncivil as strange. I beseech you, do me this courteous office, as to know of the knight what my offence to him is. It is something of my negligence, nothing of my purpose. 220
SIR TOBY	I will do so. Signior Fabian, stay you by this gentleman till my return. [*Exit*
VIOLA	Pray you, sir, do you know of this matter?
FABIAN	I know the knight is incensed against you, even to a mortal arbitrement, but nothing of the circumstance more. 225
VIOLA	I beseech you, what manner of man is he?
FABIAN	Nothing of that wonderful promise, to read him by his form, as you are like to find him in the proof of his valour. He is indeed, sir, the most skilful, bloody, and fatal opposite that you could possibly have found in any part of Illyria. Will you 230 walk towards him; I will make your peace with him if I can.
VIOLA	I shall be much bound to you for't. I am one that had rather go with Sir Priest than Sir Knight: I care not who knows so much of my mettle. [*Exeunt*

Enter **SIR TOBY** *and* **SIR ANDREW**

SIR TOBY	Why, man, he's a very devil; I have not seen such a firago. 235 I had a pass with him, rapier, scabbard and all; and he gives me the stuck in with such a mortal motion that it is inevitable. And on the answer, he pays you as surely as your feet hits the ground they step on. They say he has been fencer to the Sophy. 240
SIR ANDREW	Pox on't, I'll not meddle with him.
SIR TOBY	Ay, but he will not now be pacified: Fabian can scarce hold him yonder.
SIR ANDREW	Plague on't, an I thought he had been valiant, and so cunning in fence, I'd have seen him damned ere I'd have challenged 245 him. Let him let the matter slip, and I'll give him my horse, grey Capilet.

248	*motion*: suggestion.
249	*perdition*: loss.
251	*take up*: settle.
253	*He is ... of him*: he (i.e. Viola) is just as frightened of Sir Andrew.
255	*no remedy*: nothing to be done.
256	*for's oath sake*: for the sake of his oath.
256–7	*better ... quarrel*: thought again about the reason for his quarrel with you.
258	*draw ... vow*: draw your sword so that he can keep his vow (to fight).
	protests: promises.
260–1	*A little ... them*: it would not take much to make me tell them.
262	*Give ground*: yield.
264	*one bout*: i.e. one thrust and parry.
265	*duello*: code of rules governing the conduct of a duel.
266	*to't*: get on with it.

Antonio enters just as Cesario and Sir Andrew are about to enter into battle (line 267).

What is the dramatic significance of Antonio's entry at this point?

How does his entry affect the conspirators and the other characters?

271	*I for ... you*: challenge you on his behalf.
275	*undertaker*: one who acts on another's behalf.
	I am for you: I am ready to fight you.
275s.d.	*Officers*: the state policemen (who presumably come in from the street).
277	*I'll ... anon*: I'll see you later; Sir Toby will not fight in the presence of the Officers.
278	*put ... up*: put your sword away.
279	*Marry, will I*: I most certainly will.
	for that: as for that which.
280	*He*: i.e. 'grey Capilet'.
	reins well: goes well in a bridle.
281	*office*: duty.

SIR TOBY	I'll make the motion. Stand here, make a good show on't: this shall end without the perdition of souls.
	[*Aside*] Marry, I'll ride your horse as well as I ride you. 250

Enter **FABIAN** *and* **VIOLA**

	[*To* **FABIAN**] I have his horse to take up the quarrel; I have persuaded him the youth's a devil.
FABIAN	He is as horribly conceited of him, and pants and looks pale, as if a bear were at his heels.
SIR TOBY	[*To* **VIOLA**] There's no remedy, sir, he will fight with you 255 for's oath sake. Marry, he hath better bethought him of his quarrel, and he finds that now scarce to be worth talking of. Therefore, draw for the supportance of his vow; he protests he will not hurt you.
VIOLA	[*Aside*] Pray God defend me! A little thing would make me 260 tell them how much I lack of a man.
FABIAN	[*To* **SIR ANDREW**] Give ground if you see him furious.
SIR TOBY	Come, Sir Andrew, there's no remedy; the gentleman will for his honour's sake have one bout with you. He cannot by the duello avoid it, but he has promised me, as he is a gentleman 265 and a soldier, he will not hurt you. Come on, to't.
SIR ANDREW	Pray God he keep his oath!

Enter **ANTONIO**

VIOLA	I do assure you, 'tis against my will.

SIR ANDREW *and* **VIOLA** *draw their swords*

ANTONIO	[*Drawing*] Put up your sword! If this young gentleman Have done offence, I take the fault on me: 270 If you offend him, I for him defy you.
SIR TOBY	You, sir? Why, what are you?
ANTONIO	One, sir, that for his love dares yet do more Than you have heard him brag to you he will.
SIR TOBY	Nay, if you be an undertaker, I am for you. 275

Draws

Enter **TWO OFFICERS**

FABIAN	O good Sir Toby, hold! Here come the officers.
SIR TOBY	[*To* **ANTONIO**] I'll be with you anon.
VIOLA	[*To* **SIR ANDREW**] Pray sir, put your sword up, if you please.
SIR ANDREW	Marry, will I, sir: and for that I promised you, I'll be as good as my word. He will bear you easily, and reins well. 280
FIRST OFFICER	This is the man; do thy office.

282   *at the suit*: on the authority.

285   *favour*: face.

289   *answer it*: a) atone for it by repayment (see Act 3, Scene 3 lines 30, 35–36); b) make a defence for myself.

> Antonio is arrested and asks 'Sebastian' for his purse. 'Sebastian' claims he does not know what Antonio is talking about (lines 290–329).
>
> If you were Antonio, how would you feel when 'Sebastian' refuses to hand over your money and, worse, pretends that he does not know you?
>
> Create an online post in which you share your feelings of being used and ignored.
>
> Through this interaction Viola suspects that her brother is alive. If this is so, discuss how this might affect her. How might this affect the plot?

293   *befalls myself*: happens to me.
        amaz'd: bewildered.

294   *be of comfort*: cheer up.

296   *entreat of you*: ask you for.

299   *part*: partly.

300   *lean . . . ability*: very little money.

301   *My . . . much*: I do not have much.

302   *I'll . . . present*: I'll divide what I have now.

303   *coffer*: wealth.

304   *deny*: refuse.

305   *my deserts to you*: what I deserve from you.

306   *lack persuasion*: fail to persuade you.
        tempt: provoke.

307   *unsound*: morally weak.

308   *upbraid*: reproach.

313   *vainness*: boasting.

315   *Inhabits . . . blood*: is inherent in weak human nature.

320   *Reliev'd*: took care.
        sanctity of love: pure and intense devotion.

321   *image*: appearance.

321–2   *promise . . . worth*: show itself to be worthy of great respec

322   *did I devotion*: I worshipped.

Second Officer	Antonio, I arrest thee at the suit
	Of Count Orsino.
Antonio	You do mistake me, sir.
First Officer	No, sir, no jot: I know your favour well, 285
	Though now you have no sea-cap on your head.
	Take him away; he knows I know him well.
Antonio	I must obey. [*To* **Viola**] This comes with seeking you;
	But there's no remedy, I shall answer it.
	What will you do, now my necessity 290
	Makes me ask you for my purse? It grieves me
	Much more for what I cannot do for you,
	Than what befalls myself. You stand amaz'd,
	But be of comfort.
Second Officer	Come, sir, away. 295
Antonio	I must entreat of you some of that money.
Viola	What money, sir?
	For the fair kindness you have show'd me here,
	And part being prompted by your present trouble,
	Out of my lean and low ability 300
	I'll lend you something. My having is not much;
	I'll make division of my present with you.
	Hold, there's half my coffer.

Offers **Antonio** *money*

Antonio	Will you deny me now? [*Refuses it*]
	Is't possible that my deserts to you 305
	Can lack persuasion? Do not tempt my misery,
	Lest that it make me so unsound a man
	As to upbraid you with those kindnesses
	That I have done for you.
Viola	I know of none, 310
	Nor know I you by voice or any feature.
	I hate ingratitude more in a man
	Than lying, vainness, babbling drunkenness,
	Or any taint of vice whose strong corruption
	Inhabits our frail blood. 315
Antonio	O heavens themselves!
Second Officer	Come, sir, I pray you go.
Antonio	Let me speak a little. This youth that you see here
	I snatch'd one half out of the jaws of death,
	Reliev'd him with such sanctity of love, 320
	And to his image, which methought did promise
	Most venerable worth, did I devotion.
First Officer	What's that to us? The time goes by. Away!

325	*done . . . shame*: abused a good appearance.
326–9	*In nature . . . devil*: Antonio suddenly shifts into moralizing rhyming couplets.
327	*unkind*: a) cruel; b) unnatural.
328–9	*the beauteous . . . devil*: beautiful people who are wicked are merely empty bodies, decorated over by the devil.
333	*so do not I*: I do not believe—i.e. that what she has heard is true.
335	*ta'en*: mistaken.
337	*a couplet or two*: Sir Toby derides Antonio's sententious couplets.
	sage saws: wise sayings.
338–9	*I . . . glass*: I see a living image of my brother every time I look in the mirror.
339	*even . . . so*: exactly like this.
340	*favour*: face.
341	*Still . . . fashion*: always in clothes of this style.
344	*dishonest*: dishonourable.
	paltry: contemptible.
	a hare: A proverbial instance of cowardice.
345	*in necessity*: when he was in need.
346	*denying him*: refusing to recognise him.
	cowardship: cowardice.
347	*most . . . in it*: most sincere coward, devoted to cowardice like a religion.
348	*'Slid*: by God's eyelid.
	I'll after: I'll go after.
349	*cuff him soundly*: give him a good slap with your hand.
350	*An*: if.
351	*the event*: what will happen.
352	*lay any money*: bet any amount of money.
	yet: after all.

Class activity:

Discuss how Shakespeare highlights/portrays the theme of deception in this act.

ANTONIO	But O how vile an idol proves this god!
	Thou hast, Sebastian, done good feature shame. 325
	In nature there's no blemish but the mind:
	None can be call'd deform'd but the unkind.
	Virtue is beauty, but the beauteous evil
	Are empty trunks, o'er-flourish'd by the devil.
FIRST OFFICER	The man grows mad, away with him! Come, come, sir. 330
ANTONIO	Lead me on. *[Exit with* **OFFICERS**
VIOLA	Methinks his words do from such passion fly
	That he believes himself; so do not I!
	Prove true, imagination, O prove true,
	That I, dear brother, be now ta'en for you! 335
SIR TOBY	Come hither, knight, come hither, Fabian. We'll whisper o'er
	a couplet or two of most sage saws.
VIOLA	He nam'd Sebastian. I my brother know
	Yet living in my glass; even such and so
	In favour was my brother, and he went 340
	Still in this fashion, colour, ornament,
	For him I imitate. O if it prove,
	Tempests are kind, and salt waves fresh in love! *[Exit*
SIR TOBY	A very dishonest paltry boy, and more a coward than a hare.
	His dishonesty appears in leaving his friend here in necessity, 345
	and denying him; and for his cowardship, ask Fabian.
FABIAN	A coward, a most devout coward, religious in it!
SIR ANDREW	'Slid, I'll after him again, and beat him.
SIR TOBY	Do, cuff him soundly, but never draw thy sword.
SIR ANDREW	An' I do not— *[Exit* 350
FABIAN	Come, let's see the event.
SIR TOBY	I dare lay any money 'twill be nothing yet. *[Exeunt*

4:1

Feste and Sir Toby mistake Sebastian for Cesario and attempt to fight him, but this is interrupted by Olivia.

1	*am not sent*: have not been sent.
2	*Go to*: go away. *clear*: rid.
3	*held out*: sustained; the misunderstanding has been going on for some time.

Compare and contrast Sebastian and Viola. How are they similar? How are they different?

8	*vent*: get rid of. *of*: spoken by.
10	*lubber*: lout. *prove*: turn out to be. *cockney*: pretentious fop.
11	*ungird thy strangeness*: put off this outlandish behaviour *vent*: utter.
13	*foolish Greek*: silly clown (a 'merry Greek' = one who talks nonsense).
14	*tarry*: stay around.
15	*open*: generous; Feste remembers earlier gifts (*Act 3, Scene 1*).
16	*report*: reputation.
16–17	*after … purchase*: for a good price; the purchase-price of a piece of land was reckoned to be the sum of twelve or fourteen years' rent.
18	*There's for you*: take that.

Clearly there is a case of mistaken identity as Sir Toby and Sir Andrew encounter Sebastian.

How does the case of mistaken identity affect the plot? Outline three events that occur as a result of mistaken identity.

| 19 | *there's … there*: Sebastian probably beats Sir Andrew with the hilt of his dagger. |

4:1

The street
Enter **SEBASTIAN** *and* **FESTE**

FESTE   Will you make me believe that I am not sent for you?

SEBASTIAN   Go to, go to, thou art a foolish fellow, let me be clear of thee.

FESTE   Well held out, i' faith! No, I do not know you, nor I am not
sent to you by my lady to bid you come speak with her; nor
your name is not Master Cesario; nor this is not my nose   **5**
neither. Nothing that is so, is so.

SEBASTIAN   I prithee vent thy folly somewhere else. Thou know'st not me.

FESTE   Vent my folly! He has heard that word of some great man,
and now applies it to a fool. Vent my folly! I am afraid this
great lubber, the world, will prove a cockney. I prithee now,   **10**
ungird thy strangeness, and tell me what I shall vent to my
lady. Shall I vent to her that thou art coming?

SEBASTIAN   I prithee, foolish Greek, depart from me. There's money for
thee: if you tarry longer, I shall give worse payment.

FESTE   By my troth, thou hast an open hand. These wise men   **15**
that give fools money get themselves a good report—after
fourteen years' purchase.

Enter **SIR ANDREW**, **SIR TOBY**, *and* **FABIAN**

SIR ANDREW   Now, sir, have I met you again? There's for you!

Strikes **SEBASTIAN**

SEBASTIAN   Why, there's for thee, and there, and there!

Beats **SIR ANDREW**

     Are all the people mad?   **20**

21 *Hold*: stop.

22 *straight*: at once.

23 *coats*: places.

25 *go . . . work*: use different tactics.

26 *have . . . battery*: bring a charge of unlawful assault.

27 *its . . . that*: that won't matter.

30 *put . . . iron*: sheath your sword.
you . . . fleshed: you are eager for combat.

32 *tempt*: try.

34 *malapert*: impudent.

35 *charge*: command.

37 *Will . . . thus*: is it always going to be like this.

39 *preach'd*: taught.

41 *Rudesby*: ruffian.

43 *sway*: rule.

44 *uncivil and unjust*: barbarous and unjustified.
extent: act of violence.

46 *fruitless*: pointless.

47 *botch'd up*: patched up.
thereby: because of that.

48 *Thou . . . go*: you must go with me.

49 *deny*: refuse.
Beshrew: a (mild) curse upon.

50 *He . . . thee*: he stirred up my heart when he attacked you; Olivia alludes to the romantic notion that lovers exchange hearts with each other.
started: a) startled; b) aroused—leading to a pun on 'heart' and hart' (= deer).

51 *What . . . this*: what does this taste of (i.e. mean).
How . . . stream: what's going on.

52 *Or . . . or*: either . . . or.

53 *Let . . . steep*: let imagination for ever ('still') drown my reason in the river of forgetfulness.
Lethe: one of the rivers in the classical underworld whose waters brought total oblivion.

55 *would . . . me*: I wish you would let yourself be guided by me.

57 *say . . . so be*: say you will be so ruled, and be so indeed.

Olivia professes her love to Sebastian. Although he does not know her, he does not correct her but instead decides to go along with her (lines 54–56).

Why does Sebastian decide to go along with Olivia's plan and be 'rul'd by' her?

Discuss how the mood changes from the start of the scene to the end of the scene.

SIR TOBY	Hold, sir, or I'll throw your dagger o'er the house.
FESTE	This will I tell my lady straight. I would not be in some of your coats for twopence. *[Exit*
SIR TOBY	Come on, sir, hold!
SIR ANDREW	Nay, let him alone, I'll go another way to work with him. I'll have an action of battery against him, if there be any law in Illyria; though I struck him first, yet it's no matter for that.
SEBASTIAN	Let go thy hand!
SIR TOBY	Come, sir, I will not let you go. Come, my young soldier, put up your iron: you are well fleshed. Come on!
SEBASTIAN	I will be free from thee. What would'st thou now? If thou dar'st tempt me further, draw thy sword.

Draws

SIR TOBY	What, what! Nay, then, I must have an ounce or two of this malapert blood from you.

Draws

Enter **OLIVIA**

OLIVIA	Hold, Toby! on thy life I charge thee, hold!
SIR TOBY	Madam!
OLIVIA	Will it be ever thus? Ungracious wretch,

25

30

35

Fit for the mountains and the barbarous caves
Where manners ne'er were preach'd! Out of my sight!
Be not offended, dear Cesario. 40
Rudesby, be gone!
                    [Exeunt **SIR TOBY**, **SIR ANDREW**, *and* **FABIAN**
                    I prithee, gentle friend,
Let thy fair wisdom, not thy passion, sway
In this uncivil and unjust extent
Against thy peace. Go with me to my house, 45
And hear thou there how many fruitless pranks
This ruffian hath botch'd up, that thou thereby
May'st smile at this. Thou shalt not choose but go:
Do not deny. Beshrew his soul for me!
He started one poor heart of mine, in thee. 50

SEBASTIAN	*[Aside]* What relish is in this? How runs the stream? Or I am mad, or else this is a dream: Let fancy still my sense in Lethe steep; If it be thus to dream, still let me sleep!
OLIVIA	Nay, come, I prithee; would thou'dst be rul'd by me!
SEBASTIAN	Madam, I will.
OLIVIA	O, say so, and so be. *[Exeunt*

55

4:2

Malvolio is locked up. Feste disguises himself as a priest and treats Malvolio like a madman. Sir Toby wants to be part of the joke being played on Malvolio.

2   *Sir Topas*: The topaz, a precious stone, was believed to control lunatic passions, but Shakespeare probably takes this name from Chaucer's 'Tale of Sir Topas' (*Canterbury Tales*); 'Sir' was a complimentary title for clerics (see Act 3, Scene 4, line 233).

3   *the whilst*: meanwhile.

4   *dissemble*: disguise.

4–5   *I would*: I wish.

5   *dissembled*: pretended to be something they were not.

6   *tall*: sturdy.
     become ... well: be really impressive in this role.

7   *student*: scholar (traditionally haggard through much study).
     said: called.

8   *honest*: honourable.
     good housekeeper: hospitable man.
     goes as fairly: is just as suitable.

9   *competitors*: confederates.

11–14   *Bonos dies*: good day. In his caricature of a parson, Feste begins with bad Latin (for *bonus dies*), invents the authority of the 'hermit' ('Gorboduc' was a legendary king of England), and develops a mock-logic string of nonsense.

16   *Peace in this prison*: the greeting is prescribed in the Elizabethan *Book of Common Prayer* for the priest's entry into a sickroom.

17   *knave*: lad (used with friendly familiarity of servants).

18s.d.   *Within*: offstage.

21   *Out ... fiend*: Feste addresses the imaginary devil possessing Malvolio.
     hyperbolical: overreaching, raging.

Feste disguises himself as a priest and tries to convince Malvolio that he is crazy. Discuss the theme that Feste's disguise brings out.

27   *modest*: moderate.

28   *use*: treat.

29   *house*: room.

31   *barricadoes*: barricades (which would shut out any light).

32   *clerestories*: upper windows.
     south-north: an intentionally meaningless direction.

33   *of obstruction*: that the light is shut out.

Comment on the use and presentation of irony, humour and suspense.

36   *puzzled*: bewildered.

36–7   *the Egyptians ... fog*: A plague of 'black darkness' covered Egypt for three days (Exodus 10:21–3).

4:2

OLIVIA's *house*
Enter **MARIA** *and* **FESTE**

MARIA	Nay, I prithee put on this gown, and this beard; make him believe thou art Sir Topas the curate. Do it quickly. I'll call Sir Toby the whilst. *[Exit*
FESTE	Well, I'll put it on, and I will dissemble myself in't; and I would I were the first that ever dissembled in such a gown. 5 I am not tall enough to become the function well, nor lean enough to be thought a good student. But to be said an honest man and a good housekeeper goes as fairly as to say a careful man and a great scholar. The competitors enter.

Enter **SIR TOBY** *and* **MARIA**

SIR TOBY	Jove bless thee, Master Parson.	10
FESTE	*Bonos dies*, Sir Toby: for as the old hermit of Prague, that never saw pen and ink, very wittily said to a niece of King Gorboduc, 'That that is, is': so I, being Master Parson, am Master Parson; for what is 'that' but 'that'? and 'is' but 'is'?	
SIR TOBY	To him, Sir Topas.	15
FESTE	What ho, I say! Peace in this prison!	
SIR TOBY	The knave counterfeits well: a good knave.	
MALVOLIO	[*Within*] Who calls there?	
FESTE	Sir Topas the curate, who comes to visit Malvolio the lunatic.	
MALVOLIO	Sir Topas, Sir Topas, good Sir Topas, go to my lady!	20
FESTE	Out, hyperbolical fiend! How vexest thou this man! Talkest thou nothing but of ladies?	
SIR TOBY	Well said, Master Parson.	
MALVOLIO	Sir Topas, never was man thus wronged. Good Sir Topas, do not think I am mad. They have laid me here in hideous darkness.	25
FESTE	Fie, thou dishonest Satan! (I call thee by the most modest terms, for I am one of those gentle ones that will use the devil himself with courtesy.) Say'st thou that the house is dark?	
MALVOLIO	As hell, Sir Topas.	30
FESTE	Why, it hath bay-windows transparent as barricadoes, and the clerestories toward the south-north are as lustrous as ebony: and yet complainest thou of obstruction?	
MALVOLIO	I am not mad, Sir Topas. I say to you, this house is dark.	
FESTE	Madman, thou errest. I say there is no darkness but ignorance, in which thou art more puzzled than the Egyptians in their fog.	35

40   *abused*: badly treated.
       make the trial of it: test my sanity.

41   *constant question*: logical discussion.

42   *Pythagoras*: a Greek philosopher whose doctrine of
       the 'transmigration of souls' is correctly explained by
       Malvolio in the next line.

43   *grandam*: grandmother—i.e. ancestor.
       haply: perhaps.

45   *I think nobly*: Malvolio holds the Christian belief in the
       immortality of the soul.

47   *hold*: believe.
       allow . . . wits: certify your sanity.

48   *woodcock*: a proverbially foolish bird.
       dispossess: dislodge.

Class activity:

With the use of costumes and props, re-enact the scene with Sir Toby and
Malvolio.

From this re-enactment identify at least three emotions that Malvolio might
be experiencing as a result of his interaction with Feste. Give one reason for
each emotion identified.

---

52   *for all waters*: ready for anything.

53–4 *Thou . . . not*: The disguise had been Maria's suggestion
       (*above*, line 1).

55   *To him . . . voice*: now speak to him in your own voice.

56   *I . . . knavery*: I wish we could get this joke finished off.

57   *conveniently delivered*: released without much trouble.
       would: wish.

58   *so far in offence*: in so much trouble.

59   *upshot*: conclusion.

61   *Hey Robin*: an Elizabethan popular song.

64   *perdie*: by God (French *par Dieu*).

69   *as ever . . . hand*: if you ever want to do something for me
       which will be well rewarded.

69–70 *help me to*: fetch me.

71   *I will . . . for't*: as long as I live, I shall be grateful to you
       for this.

74   *besides*: out of.
       five wits: mental faculties: common wit, imagination,
       fantasy, judgement, and memory.

75   *notoriously abused*: shamefully ill-treated.

77   *But as well*: only as well (i.e. no better than).

MALVOLIO	I say this house is as dark as ignorance, though ignorance were as dark as hell; and I say there was never man thus abused. I am no more mad than you are—make the trial of it in any constant question.
FESTE	What is the opinion of Pythagoras concerning wildfowl?
MALVOLIO	That the soul of our grandam might haply inhabit a bird.
FESTE	What think'st thou of his opinion?
MALVOLIO	I think nobly of the soul, and no way approve his opinion.
FESTE	Fare thee well: remain thou still in darkness. Thou shalt hold th' opinion of Pythagoras ere I will allow of thy wits, and fear to kill a woodcock lest thou dispossess the soul of thy grandam. Fare thee well.
MALVOLIO	Sir Topas, Sir Topas!
SIR TOBY	My most exquisite Sir Topas!
FESTE	Nay, I am for all waters.
MARIA	Thou might'st have done this without thy beard and gown; he sees thee not.
SIR TOBY	To him in thine own voice, and bring me word how thou find'st him. I would we were well rid of this knavery. If he may be conveniently delivered, I would he were, for I am now so far in offence with my niece that I cannot pursue with any safety this sport to the upshot. Come by and by to my chamber. *[Exit with* Maria
FESTE	*Hey Robin, jolly Robin,* *Tell me how thy lady does.*
MALVOLIO	Fool!
FESTE	*My lady is unkind, perdie.*
MALVOLIO	Fool!
FESTE	*Alas, why is she so?*
MALVOLIO	Fool, I say!
FESTE	*She loves another*—Who calls, ha?
MALVOLIO	Good fool, as ever thou wilt deserve well at my hand, help me to a candle, and pen, ink, and paper. As I am a gentleman, I will live to be thankful to thee for't.
FESTE	Master Malvolio?
MALVOLIO	Ay, good fool.
FESTE	Alas, sir, how fell you besides your five wits?
MALVOLIO	Fool, there was never man so notoriously abused! I am as well in my wits, fool, as thou art.
FESTE	But as well? Then you are mad indeed, if you be no better in your wits than a fool.

Line numbers: 40, 45, 50, 55, 60, 65, 70, 75

135

79	*propertied me*: treated me like a senseless object.
80–1	*to face . . . wits*: to drive me out of my mind.
82	*Advise you*: be careful.
83–4	*thy wits . . . restore*: may the heavens restore you to your right mind.
84	*endeavour . . . sleep*: try to get some sleep.
84–5	*vain bibble babble*: meaningless prattle.
87	*Maintain no words*: don't try to talk.
88	*God buy you*: God be with you.
91	*shent*: scolded.

Consider Malvolio's statement in lines 93–94. Are all the men in Illyria really in their right minds? Justify your answer with evidence from the play.

95	*Well-a-day that*: alas, if only.
97	*convey . . . down*: carry the letter that I shall write.
97–8	*It shall . . . did*: you will get more for this than you have ever got for carrying letters.
100	*counterfeit*: pretend.
104	*requite it*: reward you for it. *in the highest degree*: to the utmost.
105–12	*'I am gone . . . devil'*: Feste's song has not been identified.
105	*anon*: at once.
107	*trice*: moment. *the old Vice*: a character in the Morality Plays of the fifteenth and sixteenth centuries, who belaboured the devil with his wooden sword and drove him from the stage.
108	*sustain*: satisfy.
111	*Pare*: cut.
112	*Adieu*: goodbye. *goodman*: good master.

MALVOLIO	They have here propertied me: keep me in darkness, send ministers to me—asses—and do all they can to face me out of my wits.

80

FESTE	Advise you what you say: the minister is here. [*Speaking as* Sir Topas] Malvolio, Malvolio, thy wits the heavens restore: endeavour thyself to sleep, and leave thy vain bibble babble.

85

MALVOLIO	Sir Topas!
FESTE	[*As* Sir Topas] Maintain no words with him, good fellow! [*As himself*] Who, I, sir? Not I, sir! God buy you, good Sir Topas! [*As* Sir Topas] Marry, amen! [*As himself*] I will, sir, I will.
MALVOLIO	Fool, fool, fool, I say!

90

FESTE	Alas, sir, be patient. What say you, sir? I am shent for speaking to you.
MALVOLIO	Good fool, help me to some light and some paper: I tell thee I am as well in my wits as any man in Illyria.
FESTE	Well-a-day that you were, sir!

95

MALVOLIO	By this hand, I am! Good fool, some ink, paper, and light, and convey what I will set down to my lady. It shall advantage thee more than ever the bearing of letter did.
FESTE	I will help you to't. But tell me true, are you not mad indeed or do you but counterfeit?

100

MALVOLIO	Believe me, I am not. I tell thee true.
FESTE	Nay, I'll ne'er believe a madman till I see his brains. I will fetch you light, and paper, and ink.
MALVOLIO	Fool, I'll requite it in the highest degree. I prithee, be gone.
FESTE	*I am gone, sir, and anon, sir,*

105

I'll be with you again,
In a trice, like to the old Vice,
Your need to sustain;
Who, with dagger of lath, in his rage and his wrath,
Cries, 'Ah, ha!' to the devil:

110

Like a mad lad, 'Pare thy nails, dad.
Adieu, goodman devil!'   *[Exit*

4:3

Sebastian is accosted by Olivia who insists that he should marry her. Although he is surprised, he seems to go along with her plans.

6   *there he was*: he had been there.
       credit: information.

7   *range*: wander around.

9   *my soul . . . sense*: my mind agrees with the evidence of my senses.

10   *this . . . madness*: there may be some mistake, but it's not madness.

11   *flood of fortune*: excess of good luck.

12   *instance*: precedent.
       discourse: explanation.

14   *wrangle*: argue.

15   *trust*: believe.

17   *sway*: govern, manage.
       followers: servants.

18   *Take . . . dispatch*: handle her household business and settle matters.

19   *With . . . bearing*: in such a calm, sensible, and poised manner.

21   *deceivable*: deceptive.

> How do you think the Duke will respond when he hears about Olivia's marriage to his servant?

> How will Olivia's marriage affect Sir Toby's and Sir Andrew's relationship?

24   *chantry*: private chapel.
       by: near by.

26   *Plight . . . faith*: Olivia is demanding a 'troth-plight' before a witness, which would constitute a legally binding contract.

27   *jealous*: possessive.
       doubtful: insecure, suspicious.

28   *He*: the 'holy man'.

29   *Whiles*: until.
       come to note: be made public.

30–1   *What . . . birth*: when we will celebrate our wedding in a manner appropriate to my social position.

32–5   *I'll . . . mine*: The romantic, rhyming couplets signal the end of an episode.

35   *fairly note*: look favourably upon.

What does this act reveal about Olivia?

List two statements that Shakespeare makes about love.

4:3

OLIVIA'*s garden*
Enter SEBASTIAN

SEBASTIAN This is the air, that is the glorious sun,
This pearl she gave me, I do feel't, and see't,
And though 'tis wonder that enwraps me thus,
Yet 'tis not madness. Where's Antonio then?
I could not find him at the Elephant. 5
Yet there he was, and there I found this credit,
That he did range the town to seek me out.
His counsel now might do me golden service:
For though my soul disputes well with my sense
That this may be some error, but no madness, 10
Yet doth this accident and flood of fortune
So far exceed all instance, all discourse,
That I am ready to distrust mine eyes,
And wrangle with my reason that persuades me
To any other trust but that I am mad, 15
Or else the lady's mad; yet if 'twere so,
She could not sway her house, command her followers,
Take and give back affairs and their dispatch,
With such a smooth, discreet, and stable bearing
As I perceive she does. There's something in't 20
That is deceivable. But here the lady comes.

Enter OLIVIA *and* PRIEST

OLIVIA Blame not this haste of mine. If you mean well,
Now go with me and with this holy man
Into the chantry by; there before him,
And underneath that consecrated roof, 25
Plight me the full assurance of your faith,
That my most jealous and too doubtful soul
May live at peace. He shall conceal it
Whiles you are willing it shall come to note,
What time we will our celebration keep 30
According to my birth. What do you say?

SEBASTIAN I'll follow this good man, and go with you,
And having sworn truth, ever will be true.

OLIVIA Then lead the way, good father, and heavens so shine,
That they may fairly note this act of mine! [*Exeunt* 35

5:1

The scene begins with a light-hearted exchange between Orsino and Feste, who 'relieves' Orsino of two coins. Antonio is arrested and brought before the Duke. Sebastian (believed to be Cesario) beats Sir Andrew and Sir Toby. The twins meet and the confusion is cleared up. Malvolio declares he's been mistreated and leaves vowing revenge. Orsino marries Viola and Sebastian marries Olivia.

1   *his*: i.e. Malvolio's letter to Olivia.

The entire act is one scene. Think about the dramatic significance of this.

As you read or perform this scene, think about the major themes and issues raised in the play. How (and to what degree) does this act address or resolve them? How are the various disguises, guises, and concealments presented?

5   *give ... again*: to give someone a gift, and ask to have it back again; see 'Source, Text, and Date', p. 14.

6   *Belong you to*: are you servants of.

7   *trappings*: ornaments.

Note how this act begins and compare it with the solemnity of the previous scene. Note that Feste is never far from the major events in the drama. What is the dramatic impact of this?

Explain Feste's opinion about friends and enemies in lines 13–24. What are your views on this issue?

13   *they*: my friends.
       make an ass: make a fool of me.

14   *plainly*: honestly.

14–15   *profit ... myself*: gain self-knowledge.
       abused: deceived, disgraced.

16   *conclusions ... kisses*: assuming that logical propositions are like kisses.

17   *your ... affirmatives*: Grammatically speaking, two negatives make an affirmative ('no "no"' = 'yes').
       your: i.e. as you know.

20   *though*: even though.

23   *But ... dealing*: except that it would be a) deceit; b) a second giving.
       I would: I wish.

26–7   *Put ... obey it*: forget your honour ('grace') for the present, and give in to your human weakness.

30   *Primo ... tertio*: first, second, third (Latin); requesting a third favour, Feste alludes to an elaborate mathematical contest, the 'Philosopher's Game'.
       the old saying: i.e. 'third time lucky'—used to encourage gamblers to make another attempt.

5:1

The street
Enter FESTE and FABIAN

FABIAN	Now as thou lov'st me, let me see his letter.
FESTE	Good Master Fabian, grant me another request.
FABIAN	Anything.
FESTE	Do not desire to see this letter.
FABIAN	This is to give a dog, and in recompense desire my dog again. **5**

Enter ORSINO, VIOLA, CURIO and LORDS

ORSINO	Belong you to the Lady Olivia, friends?
FESTE	Ay, sir, we are some of her trappings.
ORSINO	I know thee well. How dost thou, my good fellow?
FESTE	Truly, sir, the better for my foes, and the worse for my friends.
ORSINO	Just the contrary: the better for thy friends. **10**
FESTE	No, sir: the worse.
ORSINO	How can that be?
FESTE	Marry, sir, they praise me, and make an ass of me. Now my foes tell me plainly I am an ass: so that by my foes, sir, I profit in the knowledge of myself, and by my friends I am abused. **15** So that, conclusions to be as kisses, if your four negatives make your two affirmatives, why then the worse for my friends, and the better for my foes.
ORSINO	Why, this is excellent.
FESTE	By my troth, sir, no—though it please you to be one of my **20** friends.
ORSINO	Thou shalt not be the worse for me: there's gold.
FESTE	But that it would be double-dealing, sir, I would you could make it another.
ORSINO	O, you give me ill counsel. **25**
FESTE	Put your grace in your pocket, sir, for this once, and let your flesh and blood obey it.
ORSINO	Well, I will be so much a sinner to be a double-dealer; there's another.
FESTE	*Primo, secundo, tertio,* is a good play, and the old saying **30** is 'The third pays for all'; the triplex, sir, is a good tripping measure; or the bells of Saint Bennet, sir, may put you in mind—one, two, three.
ORSINO	You can fool no more money out of me at this throw. If you will let your lady know I am here to speak with her, and **35** bring her along with you, it may awake my bounty further.

31   *triplex*: triple time in music.

31–2   *tripping measure*: skipping rhythm.
Saint Bennet: St Benedict's Church stood just opposite Shakespeare's Globe Theatre.

32–3   *put you in mind*: jog your memory.

34   *fool*: trick.
throw: throw of the dice.

36   *bounty*: generosity.

37   *lullaby*: goodnight.

38–9   *my desire ... covetousness*: Feste does not explain how these are different.

40   *anon*: very soon.

44   *Vulcan*: the Roman god of blacksmiths.

> Consider lines 42–84. Viola has a different impression of Antonio than Orsino and the officers. Discuss and compare these reactions.

45   *baubling vessel*: miserable little boat.

46   *For ... unprizable*: very lightweight and not worth capturing.
draught: the depth of water needed to float a vessel.

47   *such ... make*: he engaged in such destructive close fighting.

48   *bottom*: ship.

49   *very ... loss*: even in our shame, and with the voices of losers.

50   *Cried ... him*: called out with praise and honour for him

52   *took*: captured.
fraught: freight, cargo.
Candy: Candia, capital of Crete.

55   *desperate ... state*: regardless of shame and danger.

56   *private brabble*: personal quarrel.
apprehend: arrest.

57   *drew ... side*: drew his sword in my defence.

58   *in conclusion*: afterwards.
put ... upon me: spoke very oddly to me.

59   *distraction*: madness.

60   *Notable*: notorious.
salt-water thief: robber on the seas.

61   *to their mercies*: into the hands of those men.

62   *in terms ... dear*: in such bloody and deadly circumstances.

FESTE Marry, sir, lullaby to your bounty till I come again. I go, sir, but I would not have you to think that my desire of having is the sin of covetousness. But as you say, sir, let your bounty take a nap, I will awake it anon.   [*Exit* **40**

Enter **ANTONIO** *and* **OFFICERS**

VIOLA Here comes the man, sir, that did rescue me.

ORSINO That face of his I do remember well;
Yet when I saw it last, it was besmear'd
As black as Vulcan, in the smoke of war.
A baubling vessel was he captain of,   **45**
For shallow draught and bulk unprizable,
With which such scathful grapple did he make
With the most noble bottom of our fleet,
That very envy and the tongue of loss
Cried fame and honour on him. What's the matter?   **50**

FIRST OFFICER Orsino, this is that Antonio
That took the *Phoenix* and her fraught from Candy,
And this is he that did the *Tiger* board,
When your young nephew Titus lost his leg.
Here in the streets, desperate of shame and state,   **55**
In private brabble did we apprehend him.

VIOLA He did me kindness, sir, drew on my side,
But in conclusion put strange speech upon me,
I know not what 'twas, but distraction.

ORSINO Notable pirate, thou salt-water thief,   **60**
What foolish boldness brought thee to their mercies
Whom thou in terms so bloody and so dear
Hast made thine enemies?

65   *Be ... shake off*: please allow me to deny.

67   *on base ... enough*: with very good reason.

68   *A witchcraft*: Sebastian has bewitched Antonio—just as Olivia was enchanted by Viola/Cesario (compare Act 3, Scene 1, line 102).

69   *ingrateful*: ungrateful.

70   *rude*: rough.

71   *redeem*: rescue.
     A wrack ... was: he was hopelessly shipwrecked.

73   *retention*: reservation.

74   *All ... dedication*: I completely devoted myself to him.

75   *pure*: only.

76   *adverse*: hostile.

77   *Drew*: drew my sword.
     beset: attacked.

78   *being apprehended*: when I was arrested.

79   *partake*: share.

80   *to face ... acquaintance*: brazenly to deny that he knew me.

81   *grew ... thing*: became very distant.
     removed: removèd.

82   *While ... wink*: in the twinkling of an eye.
     denied: refused to give me.

83   *recommended*: committed.

87   *three months*: Shakespeare manipulates the time schem to suit his own purposes.

88   *No int'rim*: without a break.
     vacancy: space.

89   *keep company*: stay together.

90   *heaven ... earth*: Orsino compares Olivia to a goddess.

92   *tended upon*: attended on.

93   *anon*: presently.

94   *but ... have*: except that which he may not have (i.e. Olivia's love).

95   *seem serviceable*: be of assistance.

96   *keep promise*: i.e. to be true (Act 4, Scene 3, line 33).

▌▌ *The audience sees Orsino and Olivia together for the first time. What is the dramatic impact of this meeting?*

101   *aught ... tune*: the same old stuff.

102   *fat and fulsome*: boring and sickening.

103   *howling*: the howling of a dog.

ANTONIO	Orsino, noble sir,	
	Be pleas'd that I shake off these names you give me:	65
	Antonio never yet was thief, or pirate,	
	Though I confess, on base and ground enough,	
	Orsino's enemy. A witchcraft drew me hither:	
	That most ingrateful boy there by your side,	
	From the rude sea's enrag'd and foamy mouth	70
	Did I redeem. A wrack past hope he was.	
	His life I gave him, and did thereto add	
	My love, without retention or restraint,	
	All his in dedication. For his sake	
	Did I expose myself—pure for his love—	75
	Into the danger of this adverse town;	
	Drew to defend him, when he was beset;	
	Where being apprehended, his false cunning	
	(Not meaning to partake with me in danger)	
	Taught him to face me out of his acquaintance,	80
	And grew a twenty years' removed thing	
	While one would wink; denied me mine own purse,	
	Which I had recommended to his use	
	Not half an hour before.	
VIOLA	How can this be?	85
ORSINO	When came he to this town?	
ANTONIO	Today, my lord and for three months before	
	No int'rim, not a minute's vacancy,	
	Both day and night did we keep company.	

Enter **OLIVIA** *and* **ATTENDANTS**

ORSINO	Here comes the Countess: now heaven walks on earth!	90
	But for thee, fellow—fellow, thy words are madness.	
	Three months this youth hath tended upon me;	
	But more of that anon. Take him aside.	
OLIVIA	What would my lord—but that he may not have—	
	Wherein Olivia may seem serviceable?	95
	Cesario, you do not keep promise with me.	
VIOLA	Madam?	
ORSINO	Gracious Olivia—	
OLIVIA	What do you say, Cesario? [*To* Orsino] Good my lord—	
VIOLA	My lord would speak; my duty hushes me.	100
OLIVIA	If it be aught to the old tune, my lord,	
	It is as fat and fulsome to mine ear	
	As howling after music.	
ORSINO	Still so cruel?	
OLIVIA	Still so constant, lord.	105

145

106   *uncivil*: rude, discourteous.

107   *ingrate*: ungrateful.
       unauspicious: unrewarding.

109   *e'er devotion tender'd*: ever offered in devotion.

110   *Even what*: whatever.
       become: be suitable.

112   *th' Egyptian thief*: An Egyptian bandit threatened by death
       (in a story by Heliodorus) tried to kill a captive whom he
       loved.

114   *savours nobly*: has a noble air.
       hear me this: just let me say this.

115   *to non-regardance*: into disregard.

116   *that*: since.
       partly know: have some idea of.

117   *screws*: wrests.

118   *marble-breasted*: hard-hearted.

119   *minion*: darling, favourite.

120   *tender*: hold, care for.

121   *cruel*: i.e. towards Orsino.

122   *he . . . spite*: he gets the high honour that his master
       should have.
       crowned: crownèd.

123   *ripe in mischief*: ready to do injury.

125   *a raven . . . dove*: a black heart in a fair body.

126   *jocund*: cheerful.
       apt: ready.

127   *do you rest*: give you peace.

▐ *Discuss your views on the adjectives Orsino uses to describe Olivia.*

131   *by all mores*: by all comparatives.
       love wife: love a wife.

132   *feign*: pretend.
       witnesses above: gods.

133   *tainting*: discrediting.

134   *Ay me detested*: Oh I am accursed.
       beguil'd: deceived.

135   *do you wrong*: injure you.

142   *sirrah*: a contemptuous form of address.

144   *the baseness . . . fear*: your miserable cowardice.

145   *strangle thy propriety*: suppress your real identity (i.e. as
       Olivia's husband).

146   *take . . . up*: assume your proper place in life.

147   *Be that*: be what.

148   *as that thou fear'st*: as great as the man (i.e. Orsino) that
       you are afraid of.

ORSINO	What, to perverseness? You uncivil lady,
	To whose ingrate and unauspicious altars
	My soul the faithfull'st off'rings hath breath'd out
	That e'er devotion tender'd—What shall I do?
OLIVIA	Even what it please my lord that shall become him.	110
ORSINO	Why should I not, had I the heart to do it,
	Like to th' Egyptian thief at point of death,
	Kill what I love?—a savage jealousy
	That sometimes savours nobly! But hear me this:
	Since you to non-regardance cast my faith,	115
	And that I partly know the instrument
	That screws me from my true place in your favour,
	Live you the marble-breasted tyrant still.
	But this your minion, whom I know you love,
	And whom, by heaven, I swear I tender dearly,	120
	Him will I tear out of that cruel eye
	Where he sits crowned in his master's spite.
	Come, boy, with me; my thoughts are ripe in mischief:
	I'll sacrifice the lamb that I do love,
	To spite a raven's heart within a dove.	125
VIOLA	And I most jocund, apt, and willingly,
	To do you rest, a thousand deaths would die.
OLIVIA	Where goes Cesario?
VIOLA	After him I love
	More than I love these eyes, more than my life,	130
	More, by all mores, than e'er I shall love wife.
	If I do feign, you witnesses above
	Punish my life, for tainting of my love.
OLIVIA	Ay me detested! How am I beguil'd!
VIOLA	Who does beguile you? Who does do you wrong?	135
OLIVIA	Hast thou forgot thyself? Is it so long?
	Call forth the holy father. *[Exit an Attendant*
ORSINO	Come, away!
OLIVIA	Whither, my lord? Cesario, husband, stay!
ORSINO	Husband?	140
OLIVIA	Ay, husband. Can he that deny?
ORSINO	Her husband, sirrah?
VIOLA	No, my lord, not I.
OLIVIA	Alas, it is the baseness of thy fear
	That makes thee strangle thy propriety.	145
	Fear not, Cesario, take thy fortunes up,
	Be that thou know'st thou art, and then thou art
	As great as that thou fear'st.

❚❚ *Comment on the dramatic significance of the entrance of the priest to the unfolding drama. Why might Olivia resort to call him?*

150	*charge*: order.
	by thy reverence: in all your holiness.
151	*unfold*: reveal.
	lately: recently.
152	*in darkness*: hidden.
	occasion: the circumstances.
154	*newly pass'd*: recently taken place.
156	*joinder*: joining.
157	*Attested*: demonstrated.
	the holy close of lips: a holy kiss.
158	*interchangement*: exchange.
160	*Seal'd in my function*: made official by me as a priest.
	testimony: formal statement.
161–2	*toward . . . hours*: I am only two hours older.
163	*dissembling cub*: lying little fox.
164	*sow'd . . . case*: scattered grey hairs on your head ('case' = fox-skin).
165	*craft*: cunning skill.
166	*trip*: a wrestling term for the movement that throws an opponent to the ground.
167–8	*direct . . . meet*: make sure we never meet again.
171	*Hold little faith*: keep some part of your promise.
172	*presently*: immediately.
174	*'Has . . . across*: he has hit me over the head; apparently there has been a second bout of skirmishing not shown onstage.
175	*coxcomb*: head.
175–6	*I had . . . home*: I would give a lot of money to be at home 'forty' = an unspecified large sum.

❚❚ *Note the entrance of Sir Andrew, who confuses Viola for Sebastian, lines 178–9.*

Enter **PRIEST**

	O welcome, father!	
	Father, I charge thee by thy reverence	**150**

                              O welcome, father!
Father, I charge thee by thy reverence   **150**
Here to unfold—though lately we intended
To keep in darkness what occasion now
Reveals before 'tis ripe—what thou dost know
Hath newly pass'd between this youth and me.

PRIEST   A contract of eternal bond of love,   **155**
Confirm'd by mutual joinder of your hands,
Attested by the holy close of lips,
Strengthen'd by interchangement of your rings,
And all the ceremony of this compact
Seal'd in my function, by my testimony;   **160**
Since when, my watch hath told me, toward my grave
I have travell'd but two hours.

ORSINO   O thou dissembling cub! What wilt thou be
When time hath sow'd a grizzle on thy case?
Or will not else thy craft so quickly grow   **165**
That thine own trip shall be thine overthrow?
Farewell, and take her; but direct thy feet
Where thou and I henceforth may never meet.

VIOLA   My lord, I do protest—

OLIVIA   O do not swear!   **170**
Hold little faith, though thou hast too much fear.

Enter **SIR ANDREW**

SIR ANDREW   For the love of God, a surgeon! Send one presently to Sir Toby.

OLIVIA   What's the matter?

SIR ANDREW   'Has broke my head across, and has given Sir Toby a bloody
coxcomb too. For the love of God, your help! I had rather   **175**
than forty pound I were at home.

178   *took him for*: thought he was.

179   *incardinate*: in the flesh; Sir Andrew means 'incarnate'.

181   *'Od's lifelings*: by God's little lives (a mild oath).
for nothing: for no reason.

182   *that . . . Sir Toby*: it was Sir Toby who made me do what I did.

185   *bespake you fair*: answered you courteously.

187   *set nothing by*: think nothing of.

188   *halting*: limping.
in drink: drunk.

189   *tickled . . . did*: dealt with you differently.

190   *How is't with you*: what's wrong with you.

191   *That's . . . on't*: it doesn't matter: he's hurt me, and that's tha

192   *Sot*: you drunken fool.
Dick Surgeon: Dick the surgeon.

193   *an hour agone*: for the past hour.

193–4   *set . . . morning*: glazed over (in drunkenness) at eight o'clock this morning.

195   *passy-measures pavin*: The 'passe-measure pavane' was a stately dance.

198   *be dressed*: have our wounds dressed.

200   *gull*: dupe.

201   *looked to*: taken care of.

203   *brother . . . blood*: my own brother.

204   *with . . . safety*: with any sensible concern for my own safe

205   *throw . . . me*: look upon me strangely.

207   *even for*: especially because of.

208   *but . . . ago*: so recently.

209   *One*: the same.
habit: costume; Viola explained (Act 3, Scene 4, line 341) that she imitated Sebastian in 'fashion, colour, ornament'

210   *A natural perspective*: an optical illusion produced by nature (not by mirrors).

> *Why might Sebastian say that Olivia is staring at him strangely (line 205)?*

212   *rack'd*: dragged out (as though he were tortured on the rack).

OLIVIA	Who has done this, Sir Andrew?
SIR ANDREW	The Count's gentleman, one Cesario. We took him for a coward, but he's the very devil incardinate.
ORSINO	My gentleman, Cesario? 180
SIR ANDREW	'Od's lifelings, here he is! You broke my head for nothing; and that that I did, I was set on to do't by Sir Toby.
VIOLA	Why do you speak to me? I never hurt you. You drew your sword upon me without cause, But I bespake you fair, and hurt you not. 185

Enter **SIR TOBY** *and* **FESTE**

SIR ANDREW	If a bloody coxcomb be a hurt, you have hurt me: I think you set nothing by a bloody coxcomb. Here comes Sir Toby halting; you shall hear more. But if he had not been in drink, he would have tickled you othergates than he did.
ORSINO	How now, gentleman? How is't with you? 190
SIR TOBY	That's all one; 'has hurt me, and there's th' end on't. Sot, didst see Dick Surgeon, sot?
FESTE	O, he's drunk, Sir Toby, an hour agone; his eyes were set at eight i' th' morning.
SIR TOBY	Then he's a rogue, and a passy-measures pavin. I hate a 195 drunken rogue.
OLIVIA	Away with him! Who hath made this havoc with them?
SIR ANDREW	I'll help you, Sir Toby, because we'll be dressed together.
SIR TOBY	Will you help? An ass-head, and a coxcomb, and a knave, a thin-faced knave, a gull! 200
OLIVIA	Get him to bed, and let his hurt be looked to.
	[*Exeunt* **FESTE**, **FABIAN**, **SIR TOBY**, *and* **SIR ANDREW**

Enter **SEBASTIAN**

SEBASTIAN	I am sorry, madam, I have hurt your kinsman: But had it been the brother of my blood, I must have done no less with wit and safety. You throw a strange regard upon me, and by that 205 I do perceive it hath offended you: Pardon me, sweet one, even for the vows We made each other but so late ago.
ORSINO	One face, one voice, one habit, and two persons! A natural perspective, that is, and is not! 210
SEBASTIAN	Antonio! O my dear Antonio, How have the hours rack'd and tortur'd me, Since I have lost thee!

215   *Fear'st thou*: do you doubt.

216   *made . . . yourself*: divided yourself in two.

217   *cleft*: split.

221–2   *Nor . . . everywhere*: and I don't have the divine power of being omnipresent.

223   *blind*: unseeing, pitiless.

224   *Of charity*: be kind and tell me.
kin: relation.

225   *What countryman*: what is your nationality.

228   *suited*: dressed.

229   *If spirits . . . suit*: if ghosts can appear in human form and clothing.

230–1   *spirit . . . indeed*: I certainly have an immortal soul.

232–3   *am . . . participate*: have the same physical earthly form that I was born with.

234   *as . . . even*: as it appears from everything else (except the dress).

236   *drowned*: drownèd.

239–40   *died . . . years*: died on my thirteenth birthday.

241   *record*: recollection.
lively: vivid.

242   *finished*: finishèd.
his mortal act: his life.

244   *lets*: hinders.

245   *this . . . attire*: the male clothing I have no right to wear.

247   *cohere and jump*: concur and agree.

250   *maiden weeds*: female garments.
whose: i.e. the captain's.

252   *All . . . since*: everything that has happened to me since then.

253   *between*: concerned with.

254   *So . . . mistook*: that's why you made this mistake, my lad

255   *nature . . . that*: nature corrected that mistake in her own way; the 'bias', in the game of bowls, is the lead weighting that influences the bowl's progress.

ANTONIO	Sebastian are you?	
SEBASTIAN	Fear'st thou that, Antonio?	215
ANTONIO	How have you made division of yourself?	
	An apple cleft in two is not more twin	
	Than these two creatures. Which is Sebastian?	
OLIVIA	Most wonderful!	
SEBASTIAN	Do I stand there? I never had a brother;	220
	Nor can there be that deity in my nature	
	Of here and everywhere. I had a sister,	
	Whom the blind waves and surges have devour'd.	
	Of charity, what kin are you to me?	
	What countryman? What name? What parentage?	225
VIOLA	Of Messaline. Sebastian was my father;	
	Such a Sebastian was my brother too:	
	So went he suited to his watery tomb.	
	If spirits can assume both form and suit,	
	You come to fright us.	230
SEBASTIAN	A spirit I am indeed,	
	But am in that dimension grossly clad	
	Which from the womb I did participate.	
	Were you a woman, as the rest goes even,	
	I should my tears let fall upon your cheek	235
	And say, 'Thrice welcome, drowned Viola.'	
VIOLA	My father had a mole upon his brow.	
SEBASTIAN	And so had mine.	
VIOLA	And died that day when Viola from her birth	
	Had number'd thirteen years.	240
SEBASTIAN	O, that record is lively in my soul!	
	He finished indeed his mortal act	
	That day that made my sister thirteen years.	
VIOLA	If nothing lets to make us happy both,	
	But this my masculine usurp'd attire,	245
	Do not embrace me, till each circumstance	
	Of place, time, fortune, do cohere and jump	
	That I am Viola; which to confirm	
	I'll bring you to a captain in this town,	
	Where lie my maiden weeds; by whose gentle help	250
	I was preserv'd to serve this noble Count.	
	All the occurrence of my fortune since	
	Hath been between this lady and this lord.	
SEBASTIAN	[*To* Olivia] So comes it, lady, you have been mistook.	
	But nature to her bias drew in that.	255
	You would have been contracted to a maid;	

153

257   *by my life*: upon my life.

258   *a maid and man*: a virgin youth.

259   *amaz'd*: bewildered.
        right . . . blood: he is of truly noble birth.

260   *true*: accurate, not a distorting mirror.

261   *most happy wreck*: very fortunate shipwreck.

263   *like to me*: as you love me.

264   *over-swear*: swear over again.

266   *As doth . . . fire*: as truly as the sphere of the sun
        maintains its fire.

267   *severs*: divides.

271   *action*: legal charge.

272   *in durance*: imprisoned.
        at Malvolio's suit: on the accusation of Malvolio.

273   *follower*: servant.

274   *enlarge him*: set him free.

275   *I remember me*: I remember.

276   *distract*: disturbed in his mind.

277   *A . . . own*: my own distracting madness.

280   *he holds . . . end*: he is keeping the devil ('Beelzebub') at
        the end of his staff (= at a safe distance); the metaphor is
        from fighting with staves.

281   *case*: condition.   *'Has*: he has.

282   *today morning*: this morning.

283–4   *epistles*: a) love-letters; b) Epistles of the New Testament
        of the Bible.
        gospels: a) the first four books of the New Testament;
        b) unquestionable truths.
        it . . . delivered: it doesn't matter in which order they are
        read; specific times were set in church services for the
        reading of the Gospels.

284   *delivered*: a) handed over; b) narrated.

286   *Look . . . edified*: prepare to be (spiritually) instructed.
        delivers: speaks for.

289   *do but read*: only read.
        an': if.

Nor are you therein, by my life, deceiv'd:
You are betroth'd both to a maid and man.

ORSINO   Be not amaz'd; right noble is his blood.
If this be so, as yet the glass seems true,   260
I shall have share in this most happy wreck.
[*To* Viola] Boy, thou hast said to me a thousand times
Thou never should'st love woman like to me.

VIOLA   And all those sayings will I over-swear,
And all those swearings keep as true in soul   265
As doth that orbed continent the fire
That severs day from night.

ORSINO   Give me thy hand,
And let me see thee in thy woman's weeds.

'And let me see thee in thy woman's weeds' (line 269).

VIOLA   The captain that did bring me first on shore   270
Hath my maid's garments. He upon some action
Is now in durance at Malvolio's suit,
A gentleman and follower of my lady's.

OLIVIA	He shall enlarge him: fetch Malvolio hither.
	And yet alas, now I remember me, 275
	They say, poor gentleman, he's much distract.

Enter FESTE *with a letter, and* FABIAN

	A most extracting frenzy of mine own
	From my remembrance clearly banish'd his.
	How does he, sirrah?
FESTE	Truly, Madam, he holds Beelzebub at the stave's end as well 280
	as a man in his case may do. 'Has here writ a letter to you—I
	should have given't you today morning, but as a madman's
	epistles are no gospels, so it skills not much when they are
	delivered.
OLIVIA	Open't, and read it. 285
FESTE	Look then to be well edified, when the fool delivers the
	madman. [*Reads like a madman*] By the Lord, madam—
OLIVIA	How now, art thou mad?
FESTE	No, madam, I do but read madness: an' your ladyship
	will have it as it ought to be, you must allow *vox*. 290
OLIVIA	Prithee, read i' thy right wits.
FESTE	So I do, madonna. But to read his right wits is to read thus:
	therefore, perpend, my princess, and give ear.
OLIVIA	[*To* Fabian] Read it you, sirrah.
FABIAN	[*Reads*] 295

> *By the Lord, madam, you wrong me, and the world*
> *shall know it. Though you have put me into darkness,*
> *and given your drunken cousin rule over me, yet*
> *have I the benefit of my senses as well as your*
> *ladyship. I have your own letter that induced me to* 300
> *the semblance I put on; with the which I doubt not*
> *but to do myself much right, or you much shame.*
> *Think of me as you please. I leave my duty a little*
> *unthought of, and speak out of my injury.*
> *The madly-used Malvolio* 305

OLIVIA	Did he write this?
FESTE	Ay, madam.
ORSINO	This savours not much of distraction.
OLIVIA	See him deliver'd, Fabian, bring him hither.
	[*Exit* Fabian
	My lord, so please you, these things further thought on, 310
	To think me as well a sister, as a wife;
	One day shall crown th' alliance on't, so please you,
	Here at my house, and at my proper cost.

290   *vox*: voice (Latin), the proper pitch and intonation.

291   *i' thy right wits*: in your usual way.

292   *to read . . . thus*: to read Malvolio's 'right wits' is to read like this.
his: Malvolio's.

293   *perpend*: pay attention.

298   *rule*: authority.

300   *induced*: persuaded.

301   *semblance*: appearance.

303–4   *I leave . . . unthought of*: I rather forget my manners.
out . . . injury: from my sense of injury.

308   *savours . . . distraction*: doesn't sound much like madness

309   *deliver'd*: released.

310–11   *so please . . . wife*: won't you please, now that we have thought about these matters, look on me as a sister, not a wife.

312   *One day . . . on't*: the same (wedding) day shall celebrate the relationship.

313   *proper*: own.

314   *apt*: ready.

317   *mettle*: nature.

318   *soft . . . breeding*: gentle upbringing.

322   *A sister*: Olivia will now have a sister—as well as a brother.

❚❚ What are the roles of Feste and Fabian in this scene?

327   *notorious*: outrageous.

329   *peruse*: study.

330   *hand*: handwriting.

331   *from it*: differently.
in . . . phrase: in handwriting or style.

332   *invention*: composition.

333   *grant*: admit.

334   *in the modesty of honour*: decently and honourably.

335   *clear lights*: unmistakable signs.

336   *Bade*: ordered.

338   *lighter*: inferior.

339   *acting this*: when I did this.

340   *suffer'd*: allowed.

341   *the priest*: i.e. 'Sir Topas'.

342   *geck and gull*: fool and dupe.

343   *invention*: trickery.

345   *character*: handwriting.

346   *out of question*: without a doubt.
hand: handwriting.

ORSINO	Madam, I am most apt t'embrace your offer.
	[*To* Viola] Your master quits you; and for your service 315 done him,
	So much against the mettle of your sex,
	So far beneath your soft and tender breeding,
	And since you call'd me master for so long,
	Here is my hand; you shall from this time be 320
	Your master's mistress.
OLIVIA	A sister! You are she.

Enter **FABIAN** *with* **MALVOLIO**

ORSINO	Is this the madman?
OLIVIA	Ay, my lord, this same.
	How now, Malvolio? 325
MALVOLIO	Madam, you have done me wrong,
	Notorious wrong.
OLIVIA	Have I, Malvolio? No!
MALVOLIO	Lady, you have. Pray you, peruse that letter.
	You must not now deny it is your hand: 330
	Write from it, if you can, in hand or phrase,
	Or say 'tis not your seal, not your invention.
	You can say none of this. Well, grant it then,
	And tell me, in the modesty of honour,
	Why you have given me such clear lights of favour, 335
	Bade me come smiling and cross-garter'd to you,
	To put on yellow stockings, and to frown
	Upon Sir Toby, and the lighter people?
	And acting this in an obedient hope,
	Why have you suffer'd me to be imprison'd, 340
	Kept in a dark house, visited by the priest,
	And made the most notorious geck and gull
	That e'er invention play'd on? Tell me, why?
OLIVIA	Alas, Malvolio, this is not my writing,
	Though I confess much like the character: 345
	But, out of question, 'tis Maria's hand.
	And now I do bethink me, it was she
	First told me thou wast mad; then cam'st in smiling,
	And in such forms which here were presuppos'd
	Upon thee in the letter. Prithee, be content; 350
	This practice hath most shrewdly pass'd upon thee.
	But when we know the grounds and authors of it,
	Thou shalt be both the plaintiff and the judge
	Of thine own cause.
FABIAN	Good madam, hear me speak, 355
	And let no quarrel, nor no brawl to come,

347	*bethink me*: remember.
348	*then cam'st*: then you came.
349	*forms*: ways.
	presuppos'd: earlier enjoined.
351	*This . . . thee*: this trick has been played on you most mischievously.
352	*grounds*: reasons.
	authors: those responsible.

> Olivia is not angry when she learns that Maria had misrepresented her and forged her signature in the letter. What does that tell you about her character and her attitude towards Maria?

356	*to come*: in future.
357	*Taint*: spoil.
	condition: happiness.
358	*wonder'd*: marvelled.
360	*Set . . . against*: played this trick on Malvolio.
361–2	*Upon . . . him*: because of some harsh and discourteous behaviour we had attributed to him.
	writ: wrote.
363	*importance*: importunity.
364	*In recompense whereof*: as a reward for which.
365	*How . . . follow'd*: how it was carried out like a naughty game.
366	*pluck on*: provoke.
367	*If that*: if.
	justly: fairly.
368	*pass'd*: been suffered.
369	*baffled*: humiliated.
372	*interlude*: entertainment.
	one Sir Topas: a certain Sir Topas.
	that's all one: that isn't important.
374–5	*'Madam . . . gagged'*: Feste recalls Malvolio's words early in the play (Act 1, Scene 5, lines 70–74).
375	*whirligig*: spinning-top.
	his: its.
378	*notoriously abus'd*: shamefully misused.
380	*the captain*: the captain who keeps Viola's 'maiden weeds' (line 250).
381	*convents*: is convenient.
382	*solemn combination*: formal union.
383	*sweet sister*: Orsino accepts Olivia's invitation (lines 311–312).

'Alas, Malvolio, this is not my writing' (line 344).

	Taint the condition of this present hour,	
	Which I have wonder'd at. In hope it shall not,	
	Most freely I confess, myself and Toby	
	Set this device against Malvolio here,	360
	Upon some stubborn and uncourteous parts	
	We had conceiv'd against him. Maria writ	
	The letter, at Sir Toby's great importance,	
	In recompense whereof he hath married her.	
	How with a sportful malice it was follow'd	365
	May rather pluck on laughter than revenge,	
	If that the injuries be justly weigh'd	
	That have on both sides pass'd.	
OLIVIA	Alas, poor fool, how have they baffled thee!	
FESTE	Why, 'Some are born great, some achieve greatness, and	370
	some have greatness thrown upon them.' I was one, sir, in	
	this interlude, one Sir Topas, sir—but that's all one.	
	'By the Lord, fool, I am not mad.' But do you remember:	
	'Madam, why laugh you at such a barren rascal; an' you smile	
	not, he's gagged'? And thus the whirligig of time brings in his	375
	revenges.	
MALVOLIO	I'll be reveng'd on the whole pack of you! [*Exit*	
OLIVIA	He hath been most notoriously abus'd.	
ORSINO	Pursue him, and entreat him to a peace.	
	He hath not told us of the captain yet. [*Exit* Fabian	380
	When that is known, and golden time convents,	
	A solemn combination shall be made	
	Of our dear souls. Meantime, sweet sister,	

386	*habits*: clothes (i.e. her female dress).
387	*fancy's*: love's.
388	*When ... and*: when I was only.
390	*A foolish ... toy*: a silly trick was accepted as something trivial.
392	*came to man's estate*: grew up to be a man.
396	*to wive*: to take a wife.

Why might it be dramatic to have Orsino as the last to speak before the curtain falls on Feste's song?

400	*came ... beds*: got much older.
402	*With ... heads*: like other drunkards I always had a hangover.
406	*that's all one*: that doesn't matter now.
407	*we'll strive ... day*: the signal for the audience to applaud.

Comment on the effect of repetition in Feste's song. As an audience member how might this appeal to you as the play reaches its conclusion?

We will not part from hence. Cesario, come—
For so you shall be while you are a man.   **385**
But when in other habits you are seen.
Orsino's mistress, and his fancy's queen.

                    [Exeunt all except Feste

FESTE   *When that I was and a little tiny boy,*
            With hey, ho, the wind and the rain,
        A foolish thing was but a toy,   **390**
            For the rain it raineth every day.

        But when I came to man's estate,
            With hey, ho, the wind and the rain,
        'Gainst knaves and thieves men shut their gate,
            For the rain it raineth every day.   **395**

        But when I came, alas, to wive,
            With hey, ho, the wind and the rain,
        By swaggering could I never thrive,
            For the rain it raineth every day.

        But when I came unto my beds,   **400**
            With hey, ho, the wind and the rain,
        With toss-pots still 'had drunken heads,
            For the rain it raineth every day.

        A great while ago the world begun,
            With hey, ho, the wind and the rain,   **405**
        But that's all one, our play is done,
            And we'll strive to please you every day.

                            [Exit

The Songs in *Twelfth Night*

`O mistress mine' is from Act 2, Scene 3 when Sir Toby and Sir Andrew encourage Feste to sing a love song. `When I was just a boy' is also sung by Feste. This comes at the end of the play when all the other actors exit.

Suggested activity

Use the same words and create your own music for these songs or translate these songs into your own nation language (Creole).

O mistress mine

When that I was

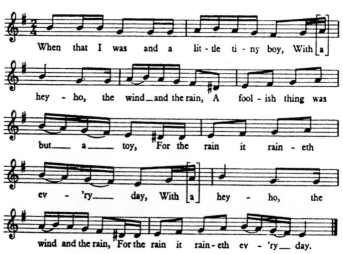

Exploring *Twelfth Night* in the Classroom

Twelfth Night is a play about love, disguises, misunderstandings, mischief and fun. Like the best comedies, it works on different levels and it has something for all ages, so students will find plenty to enjoy in this play.

This section will suggest a range of approaches in the classroom, to help bring the text to life and to engender both enjoyment and understanding of the play.

Ways into the Play

Students may feel an antipathy towards the study of Shakespeare. The imaginative and enthusiastic teacher, with the help of this edition of the play, will soon break this down!

Twelfth Night

The Christian feast of Epiphany, Twelfth Night, is the day we associate with the Christmas tree coming down and decorations being put away. It's the last day of the Christmas season of festivities and therefore a last opportunity to make merry and have fun. Ask students to consider the types of ingredients that would be suitable for a play being performed at this time of year.

Every picture tells a story

Ask your students to look at some pictures related to *Twelfth Night* – for example, the picture on the front cover of this book, or some paintings or photos on the internet – and guess who the people are and what is happening. Once they are more familiar with the play, ask them to hazard a guess as to the exact moment in the play that is depicted.

Navigating the play

Your students may need some help and practice in finding their way around a Shakespeare play. After explaining the division into acts, scenes and lines, challenge them to look up some references as quickly as possible. Refer them to some of the famous lines and those that might lead on to further discussion of the plot. Below are some suggestions:

	Act 1
Scene 1, line 1	(*If music be the food of love, play on*)
	Act 1
Scene 3, line 2	(*I am sure care's an enemy to life*)

	ACT 2
SCENE 5, LINES 119–121	(*Some are born great, some achieve greatness, and some have greatness thrust upon 'em*)
	ACT 3
SCENE 4, LINES 108–109	(*If this were played upon a stage now, I could condemn it as an improbable fiction*)

Improvisation

Working on one of these improvisations may help students access some of the ideas behind the drama.

a) Ask students to work in threes to create a short improvisation, perhaps based on a current soap opera, in which character A fancies character B, but B fancies C, and C fancies A! How do they behave and react to each other?

b) Ask students to work in small groups. Two of them should take on the part of identical twins. The group should work out a short improvisation in which misunderstandings and chaos arise due to mistaken identities with the twins.

c) Working in small groups, the students should create a scene in a work setting. One of the characters is pompous, bossy and self-important. How do the rest of the characters decide to react towards this character?

Setting the Scene

Comedy

Twelfth Night is a comedy, mainly about romance. The comedic ingredients of the play include twins, unwelcome drunken guests, pompous and love-sick characters. Ask your students what sort of situations they will expect to find in such a play. Not all the romances run smoothly, and there are many misunderstandings. Discuss whether we find the same sort of situations in modern comedies.

The music of love

The opening line of the play is possibly the most famous of Shakespeare's opening lines. It points out the intertwined relationship between love and music. Ask students to consider what the idea refers to and whether music is still the food of love today (e.g. love is featured in pop music, and couples often have a 'special' song). Finally, ask students to consider the different ways in which love is reflected in music.

Illyria

The play is set on an ancient part of the Adriatic coast, which is probably intended as a romantic, faraway, dreamy landscape. Ask students to imagine that they have just arrived on the coast after being shipwrecked. Working in pairs, one should give the other (whose eyes are closed) a guided tour of the coast. The tour could either involve students moving around if you have room, or seated. They should comment on what they can see, hear, and feel in the environment, before swapping roles and continuing the guided tour as they imagine venturing inland.

Keeping Track of the Action

It's important to give students opportunities to 'digest' and reflect upon their reading, so that they may take ownership of the play.

Reading journal

As you read through the play, help students to trace and understand the story by asking them to keep a journal in which they record what happens. They can also record their reactions and thoughts about the action and the characters. Help them to keep their responses focused by giving them specific questions to answer.

Horoscopes

Astrology is mentioned by some of the characters in the play (e.g. Act 1, Scene 3, line 112). Ask students to write horoscopes for different characters at various points in the action. Suitable points in the play are:

- Act 1, Scene 2   Viola – what lies ahead after the shipwreck and loss of her brother?
- Act 1, Scene 5   Olivia – a new person enters her life
- Act 2, Scene 5   Malvolio – all is not as it seems
- Act 4, Scene 1   Sebastian – watch out for newcomers
- Act 5, Scene 1   Orsino – a familiar person has hidden depths.

Ideally, the horoscopes should contain some ambiguity, as well as reflect the students' grasp of the plot and characters.

Twelfth Night

Court news

Ask students to write regular bulletins for Orsino's *Court News*. This is a bulletin that tracks the comings and goings at court (e.g. Cesario's arrival) and in the local area (e.g. Sir Andrew's visit), gives up-to-date news on local people of importance (e.g. Olivia), a diary of entertainment and events (e.g. Feste's songs), and gossip about events in the area (e.g. the strange behaviour of Malvolio).

Characters

Students of all ages need to come to an understanding of the characters: their motivations, their relationships, and their development.

Names

Shakespeare often gives clues about the characters in their names. Malvolio, for example, is derived from the Latin 'mal', meaning 'bad', and 'volio' meaning 'I wish'. Sir Toby Belch reminds us of a fat little toby jug and a rather loud burp. Sir Andrew Aguecheek's name derives from 'ague', meaning fever. Ask students to draw cameos of the main characters.

Casting director

Ask your students to cast the parts for a new film or stage version of *Twelfth Night*. First, they will need to construct a profile on the characters, containing information about them (known and surmised). Next, they must make a report on who they are going to invite to take on the parts, and why. Finally, they should give each actor important information about his or her character, and suggestions on how to play the part.

A different perspective

Allowing your students the opportunity to think, write, and talk as one of the characters gives them a new and illuminating perspective on the character(s). Here are some possible tasks:

- Act 1, Scene 3   Sir Andrew creates a video for a dating agency, looking for a partner
- Act 1, Scene 5   Olivia writes a letter to Cesario after their first meeting
- Act 2, Scene 3   Maria writes down her plan to trick Malvolio
- Act 2, Scene 4   Orsino composes a song about what love is like
- Act 5, Scene 1   Antonio explains why he was Orsino's enemy.

Themes

Love

We see different kinds of love, and different attitudes towards love in this play. Ask students to see if they can find evidence of any of the following:

- a man who loves the idea of being in love
- a woman whose love is hidden
- a man who loves himself
- sibling love
- love of friends.

Students could look for other examples of how love is portrayed in the play, and to consider who shows the deepest and most sincere love. Ask for volunteers to take on some of the roles and 'hot seat' them, asking them about their views on love.

Appearances

Outward appearances often fool the main characters in the play. Consider how the following characters are fooled by appearances at different points in the play:

- Olivia
- Orsino
- Sir Andrew
- Malvolio
- Antonio.

Do any of the characters remain clear-sighted throughout the play?

Deception

The play is mostly light-hearted with little malice or real wrong doing. There are deceptions, though, including Viola disguising herself as Cesario and Sir Toby's manipulation of Sir Andrew. The person who seems to come off worst, and who is not reconciled by the end of the play, is Malvolio. Discuss whether the deception involving Malvolio is deserved or 'over the top'.

Gender and sexual identity

In several instances Shakespeare seems to challenge the stereotypes held about gender. He also highlights the disparity in power which exists between males and females in Elizabethan society.

Master-servant relationship

The desire to subvert the master-servant relationship can be seen in Malvolio's ideas about himself and the place he thinks he should occupy in Olivia's heart and household. It can also be seen in the way Maria seeks to manipulate matters concerning Olivia.

The actions of these characters are consistent with the reversal of roles which often took place during the festivities that occur in the twelve nights following Christmas. Can you think of any other examples of where the existing order seems to be subverted?

Shakespeare's Language

Prose and verse

Shakespeare uses prose and verse for different reasons. In this play prose, often the preserve of common characters, is used for the comedy scenes, while verse is used for the more serious and elevated language. Ask students to investigate which characters talk mainly in verse, which in prose, and which characters use both. Challenge them to identify why either verse or prose is used at a particular point.

Imagery

As this play is primarily concerned with love, there are many images that relate to different aspects of love. Love is something to be sought, but it is also the cause of pain and distress. Ask students to look at how the characters describe love, and what they compare it with. For example, look at the speech of the following characters:

- Orsino in Act 1, Scene 1
- Viola in Act 1, Scene 5
- Orsino and Viola in Act 2, Scene 4.

Songs

As well as the verse and prose, the play contains songs which are sung by Feste. These tend to have a sad or reflective tone when discussing love. Ask students to study Feste's style of verse (e.g. the regular rhythm and rhyme), and then to create a poem summing up the events of the play.

Exploring with Drama

Book the hall or push back the desks, because the best way to study a great play is through drama. Students of all ages will benefit from a dramatic encounter with *Twelfth Night*. They will enjoy the opportunity to act out a scene or two, or to explore the situations through improvisation, for example, by putting a character in the 'hot seat' for questioning by others.

Conscience corridor

Viola is in disguise and working for the Duke. Although she has fallen in love with him, she finds herself taking his messages of love to another woman. Ask one student to play the role of Viola, while the rest of the class forms two lines facing each other, making a corridor. One side of the corridor will advise Viola to be honourable and take the messages; the other side of the corridor will urge her to throw aside her disguise and declare her love for him. Viola must walk down the corridor seeking advice. As she passes each student, they will urge her to take their guidance. Once she reaches the end, she must decide what to do.

Tableaux

Ask your students to create a tableau, or freeze-frame, in groups, involving all the main characters in the play. The characters should be grouped together according to their relationships and positions within the play. Bring the tableaux to life briefly, by having each person say something in character.

Comedy acting

Above all else, this play is a comedy. Let students enjoy acting out a comedy scene from the play, for example, Act 3, Scene 4, lines 1–56. Ask students to take on a character from the chosen scene, and appoint one student as the director. The director must then interpret and lead the other students to give an action reading of the scene – they can use their scripts but must act out the lines. Encourage them to use timing, actions, voices and expressions to bring out the comedy of the scene.

Writing about *Twelfth Night*

If your students have to write about *Twelfth Night* for coursework or for examinations, you may wish to give them this general guidance:

- Read the question or task carefully, highlight the key words, and answer all parts of the question.
- Planning is essential. Plan what will be in each paragraph. You can change your plan if necessary.
- Avoid retelling the story.
- *Twelfth Night* is a play – so consider the impact or effect on the audience.
- Keep quotations short and relevant.
- Avoid referring to a film version of the play, unless this is part of your task.

Exam-style questions

1. '*Twelfth Night* can be seen as a commentary on social stratifications in society.'

   Write an essay in which you describe two examples of class structures at work. For one of these examples, show how a character is impacted by this. Show how Shakespeare uses a dramatic technique to portray this issue.

2. 'Although serious issues are ventilated in the play, *Twelfth Night* can also be seen as a light-hearted comedy.'

   Write an essay in which you describe two incidents/events that can be considered light-hearted and discuss the impact of one of those incidents/events. Show how Shakespeare uses humour to engender audience appeal.

3. 'In *Twelfth Night*, the soliloquies are authentic tools that connect characters with the audience.'

   Write an essay in which you select and describe one soliloquy, showing how it is used to advance the drama. Discuss the use of soliloquies as a dramatic technique in this play.

4. 'Music not only enhances the theme but has a dramatic function in *Twelfth Night*.'

   Write an essay in which you describe two instances in which music is presented and discuss the effect of one. Additionally, show how music is used to introduce or reinforce a theme in the play.

5. 'One of the most appealing elements of this play is the exploration of unrequited love.'

   Write an essay in which you describe two instances of unrequited love in the play and show how a major character is affected by this. Show how Shakespeare uses a dramatic device to present this theme.

6. 'Feste is no fool. He is one of the most insightful characters in the play.'

   Write an essay in which you describe Feste's interaction with two characters in the play and discuss the response of one of the characters you have described. Discuss one dramatic device used to present Feste's function in the play.

7. '*Twelfth Night* presents a cast with a healthy mix of characters who inject real-life situations into the drama.'

   Write an essay in which you describe two characters that appear to be different from each other. Discuss their role in the drama and show how Shakespeare uses contrast as a dramatic technique in this play.

8. 'The issue of desire features prominently in *Twelfth Night*.'

   Write an essay in which you describe two instances in which a character yearns for something or someone and discuss the outcome of one of these instances. Show how Shakespeare uses a dramatic technique to portray this issue.

9. 'In *Twelfth Night,* the audience is treated to various kinds of relationships.'

   Write an essay in which you describe one relationship. Discuss the attitude of one of the characters to the other and show how Shakespeare uses suspense to portray relationships as a whole.

10. 'To some degree, Viola and Maria defy stereotypical presentation of women of that period.'

    Write an essay in which you describe in detail either Viola or Maria and discuss how their actions influence an outcome in the play. Show how Shakespeare uses a dramatic technique to present or represent women.

11. 'Gender issues are raised in Shakespeare's *Twelfth Night*.'

    Write an essay in which you describe a situation in which one gender issue is raised. In this essay you must discuss how this situation impacts the life of one major character and examine one theme that the playwright uses to highlight this issue.

12. 'The theme of Deception can be seen throughout *Twelfth Night*.'

    Write an essay in which you describe an incident where deception is evident. In this essay you must also discuss how this deception impacts the lives of two characters and explain how it affects the plot.

13. 'In Shakespeare's *Twelfth Night* things are not always what they appear to be.'

    Write an essay in which you describe two instances where things are not what they initially appear to be. In this essay you must also discuss how these two instances might have affected the audience and examine one theme that Shakespeare uses to bring out appearance versus reality.

14. 'Although Maria is insignificant in this society, she plays a significant role in *Twelfth Night*.'

    Write an essay in which you outline the role that Maria has in the play. In this essay you must also discuss how Maria's actions impact the plot and examine how her role aligns with the celebrations which take place during this period of merrymaking.

15. 'Love seems to drive many of the characters' actions in *Twelfth Night*.'

    Write an essay in which you describe a situation when one major character acts out of love. In this essay you must also discuss how this act of love is likely to impact this character's life and examine one device that Shakespeare uses to highlight this theme.

16. '*Twelfth Night* has several characters who want to escape their reality.'

    Write an essay in which you describe how one major character tries to escape his or her reality. In this essay you must discuss the reasons why this character attempts to escape and examine one dramatic technique that is used to execute this escape.

17. 'Shakespeare uses costumes as a tool to drive the plot in *Twelfth Night*.'

    Write an essay in which you describe how costumes are used in two situations. In this essay you must discuss how the use of these costumes affects the plot. You must also explain how this might have impacted the audience.

18. 'It is fitting that *Twelfth Night* ends with a song. It concretises the light-hearted mood that runs throughout the play.'

    Write an essay in which you describe an event that produces a light-hearted mood. In this essay you must discuss how this mood would affect the audience and examine a device that Shakespeare uses to create this mood.

19. 'Although Malvolio thinks highly of himself, the other characters do not.'

    Write an essay in which you describe a situation where Malvolio's conceit can be seen. In this essay you must discuss how the actions of the other characters show their disrespect for Malvolio and explain how humour is used to highlight this situation.

20. 'Knights are supposed to be honourable, but the actions of Sir Toby and Sir Andrew are contrary to this view.'

Write an essay in which you describe one dishonourable action of each knight. In this essay you must discuss why these actions are not typical of knights' behaviour. Further, you must examine one device that Shakespeare uses to portray this atypical behaviour.